THE
TAOIST SECRETS
OF
LONG LIFE
AND
GOOD HEALTH

THE
TAOIST SECRETS
OF
LONG LIFE
AND
GOOD HEALTH

A COMPLETE PROGRAMME
TO REJUVENATE MIND, BODY AND SPIRIT

Charles Chan

A GODSFIELD BOOK
www.godsfieldpress.com

First published in Great Britain in 2006 by Godsfield Press,
a division of Octopus Publishing Group Ltd
2–4 Heron Quays, London E14 4JP

Distributed in the United States and Canada by
Sterling Publishing Co., Inc.
387 Park Avenue South, New York, NY 10016–8810

1 3 5 7 9 10 8 6 4 2

Printed and bound in China

ISBN-13: 9781841812816
ISBN: 1 84181 281 1

CONTENTS

INTRODUCTION

It is everyone's dream to be eternally youthful and to live for ever. For over 5,000 years, similar to Indian yoga of the Hindu tradition, Taoists in China have devised and perfected the Immortal Alchemy techniques and harmonious ways of living to promote good health and longevity. Taoists believe that a natural human life span should be between 120 and 180 years. Some Immortals were known to have lived well over 300 years and beyond.

Today, however, our boundless desires and unrealistic expectations, together with frequent impetuous actions, excessive indulgence in external stimuli (such as drugs, coffee or tobacco) and extreme emotional upheaval, lead to a psychosomatic energy imbalance. Such an imbalance causes depletion of our vital life force leading to illness and shortening of life expectancy. In fact, Taoists do not consciously pursue extended youthfulness and longevity. They are merely the by-products of spiritual cultivation and holistic living. Taoists treat body, mind and spirit as an integral entirety. The pathway of attaining spiritual enlightenment must involve strengthening the physical body, promoting emotional equilibrium and cultivating spiritual growth.

HARMONIOUS LIVING

Taoism has been the foundation system of the Chinese culture since antiquity. Its principles manifest in most facets of everyday life for the Chinese, including philosophy, arts, cuisine, science, cosmology, healing arts, martial arts and spiritual cultivation. At the heart of Taoism is the trinity of harmony, that is man, earth (nature) and heaven (universe). If man can harmonize himself with his environment and the universe, he can maximize his full potential to live a long, happy and productive life.

To cultivate such harmony, Taoists devised the harmonization principles of Yin and Yang (the two aspects of complementary opposites in Chinese philosophy), the Five Elements (earth, wood, fire, metal and water) and the eight trigrams. A trigram is a figure made up of three lines, symbolizing the trinity of heaven, earth and man. These principles govern the synchronization of the universal energy Qi. Qi is the Chinese romanized spelling of Chi. In the Chinese alphabets Q is pronounced as a CH sound. Qi bears a similar concept to the Hindu word Prana or the Greek word Pneuma. Qi is the primal creative energy, which permeates throughout the Universe.

The level of Qi within our body governs the balance and the wellbeing of our body, mind and spirit. When Qi is abundant and in harmony, it reflects in good health, happiness and a high capacity for fulfilment. When Qi is low and sluggish, it reflects in ill health, lack of motivation, sadness or depression. By adopting a holistic lifestyle and by practising the appropriate exercises and meditation techniques, we can invoke a sequence of energy transformations physically, psychically and spiritually. If we are committed to following such a pathway, we can command good health, longevity, expanded creative potentials and profound spiritual happiness.

BECOMING AN IMMORTAL

Taoist Immortal Practices can free us from excessive desire, unrealistic expectations, emotional upheaval, negativity, ignorance, prejudice, ill health and the fear of death. When we are truly free and emancipated, we will become an Immortal. An Immortal is a peaceful, tolerant, non-judgemental, warm and loving human being who has deep spiritual understanding and empathy toward others and nature. A selfless human being acquires high purposes, noble inspirations and a great capacity for positive fulfilment in giving, healing, sharing, creating, enjoying and beautifying life for themselves and others.

This book reveals the Taoist forgotten, esoteric, secret arts of Alchemy Meditation, complementary exercises and holistic living. These secrets have enabled my extended youthfulness, abundant vitality, excellent health and profound spiritual happiness. Although I am 52 years old, physically I look and feel 20 years younger. Psychologically, I am ageless, and spiritually, I have the most profound eternal happiness within my consciousness. Taoist philosophy is a universal wisdom, which has no cultural, social, intellectual or religious ties. Hence, this book is written for all people in the world who are seeking the

wisdom of holistic health, harmonious living or deeper spiritual understanding to enrich their lives. I hope this book will also help you to gain happiness, good health, longevity and spiritual enlightenment. This book is a modern adaptation of Taoist esoteric arts of Immortal Practices. It is a complete programme for rejuvenation, health, emotional equilibrium and spiritual cultivation.

TAOISM AND THE IMMORTAL PRACTICES

The next chapter introduces Taoism, the pathway to Immortality. It intentionally gives you an induction into Taoism, the macro concepts behind Taoist spiritual cultivation and Immortal Practices. It also gives you some guidelines to help you understand the nature of the programme and how to use this book.

The chapter provides a background understanding of the Immortal Practices. It also prepares you with a more in-depth philosophical understanding concerning the meaning of Tao and its fundamental harmonizing principles of Yin and Yang, the Five Elements, known as Wu Xing, and the eight trigrams or Pa Kua. The philosophy of Lao Tzu and Chuang Tzu will provide you with spiritual food for thought. Philosophy must not be read and understood literally. The lack of clarity is intentionally used to inspire and elucidate your deeper level of understanding. True wisdom is beyond words or intellectual rationality.

THE IMMORTALITY PROGRAMME

The next section is the Immortality Programme. This introduces you to various exercises and practices such as Deep Relaxation, meditation and yoga exercises. Deep Relaxation is the preparatory phase of the Alchemy Meditation. It involves profound physical relaxation and sharpens the focus of the mind to induce pure thought. Take note of the details of posture, clothing and meditation environment.

Read the instructions thoroughly before performing the meditation routines. You don't need to learn and perform all of the routines at once. Learn and do a few steps a time. Pay attention to following the sequence of visualization correctly and the small details of how to position your head and your body.

This is followed by yoga-like exercises. There are nine exercises altogether, which are performed both before and after the meditation. Traditionally, face massage (Ca Mian), back massage (Mo Bei) and Dan Tien massage (Mo Dan Tien) are performed before the meditation to activate Qi movement and increase the body's awareness. Dan Tien is located at the lower abdominal area. You can certainly perform these exercises independently as your daily workout.

The Heavenly Primal Elixir Meditation comes next. This Taoist Alchemy meditation will revitalize the psychic centres and transform the physical, psychic and spiritual energies to rejuvenate the body and liberate the spirit. Do this meditation only when you have made positive progress with the inductive meditation of Deep Relaxation. You will need to understand and utilize the principle of non-action (Wu Wei). You will also need to familiarize yourself with the locations of the psychic centres along the meridians. It is essential to have full body awareness while putting all your concentration onto your Dan Tien area.

THE LIVING TAO

The last section looks into the modern adaptation of Taoist holistic living. The first chapter is divided into three main categories: food and drink, physical exercise and a healthy environment. You can study a small section at a time and put the knowledge into action in your everyday life. A chapter providing some classical formulas for enhancing health and aiding the meditation practice follows. Ginseng and Dong Quai are particularly valuable for strengthening your body and balancing the energy. The blood purifier/ detoxifier can be used liberally during a fasting period. Study the preparation methods and make sure you use the correct utensils for processing.

Finally, the last chapter shows you how to cultivate spiritual immortality. It explains the Taoist theories, principles and practices that can be utilized in your everyday life so as to make a life-changing experience for your physical, emotional and spiritual wellbeing. In order to earn the maximum benefit from this chapter, you need to study all the preceding chapters first. This chapter will show you how to set goals, expand your full creative potential, harmonize your environment, improve your relationships with your friends and family and live a philosophical and spiritual life.

UNDERSTANDING TAOISM AND THE IMMORTAL PRACTICES

Along with Confucianism, Taoism is the oldest and most influential indigenous foundation system of the Chinese culture. While Confucianism is a manmade system, Taoism is based on the observation of nature.

Although Confucianism served its purpose in setting the ethical and hierarchical orders in ancient feudalistic China, it carried a lot of unresolved problems. Absolute submission to the elders and to authority has no place in the democratic world today. For centuries women and the poor castes were made victims of discrimination as a direct result of blindly following the Confucian ethic.

Taoism is a timeless and boundless universal wisdom. Apart from permeating deeply into the Chinese consciousness and the Chinese culture since antiquity, it continuously inspires contemporary eastern and western thinkers alike. Relativistic physicist Albert Einstein and quantum physicist Niels Bohr were both intrigued and inspired by the profound wisdom of Taoism. Taoism can withstand the test of time because its fundamental principles are based on universal truth. If man works according to the natural rhythm of the universe and adapts to its changes, he can develop great harmony within himself and with nature. Taoist principles can be applied to all human situations including relationships and human interactions, business and management, politics and diplomacy, health and medicine, science and technology, environment and ecology.

Taoism is based on intuitive understanding. Meditation is the means to bridge over such understanding. Words and symbols are used to communicate and interpret the philosophy of the meditative insights. To fully understand Taoism we need to surpass our intellectual interpretation and see beyond everyday rationality. Unlike western thoughts, Chinese thoughts are non-linear, non-directive, flexible and nebulous because they often act as pointers to elucidate and to inspire spiritual insight. Understanding Taoist philosophy is thus an indispensable catalyst for inaugurating the Alchemy Meditation and Immortal Practices.

WHAT IS TAOISM?

The word Tao is commonly mispronounced as Ta-o. It should be pronounced phonetically as Dao with only one syllable. As this phonetic interpretation (Tao) has been universally recognized and has appeared in all major English dictionaries, I therefore adhere to the word Tao instead of Dao in this book. Tao literally means the way or the truth, which coincidentally is synonymous with the proclamation of Christ, 'I am the way, the truth and the life.' Indeed, Tao encompasses all of these qualities and beyond because Tao is the origin of all things (Reality) and nothingness (Void), the mother of the cosmic duality. Tao itself is nameless, empty, formless, silent, and yet it is all-encompassing, self-generative, inexhaustible, eternally active and eternally transforming.

Like many great schools of thought and religions in the world, the purity of Taoism has been profaned by the interpolation of folklore, superstition and shamanic practices. During the Eastern Han Period (25–220 CE) Taoist religious sects emerged. Since the introduction of Zen teaching by Buddha Dharma in 520 CE, the shamanic Taoist religious sects (Tao Jiao) have heavily borrowed from its religious and ritualistic practices. Consequently, Taoist religion evolved into a polytheistic religion; characters from folklore and fairytales together with Sakyamuni Buddha and Kuan Yin (Avalokitesvara Boddhisattva) were worshipped as their newly founded deities.

Taoism in its original and pure form has no theistic connotation at all. The name Tao does not equate to God as in other theistic religions. The word Tao itself has no intrinsic meaning, it is just a borrowed vehicle to represent the indescribable universal procreative phenomena. The name Tao was a human creation and the person who created the name Tao was also one of the creations from the creator, Tao. It is for this reason Lao Tzu taught us to see beyond the word/name and not to be confused by the creation as the creator.

Tao can be spoken which is not the usual Tao. Its name can be spoken which is not the usual name.

TAO TE JING

Principles, Beliefs and Symbols

In order to interpret the Taoist sages' meditative insights and observations, their principles and beliefs, a number of symbols were introduced. Tai Chi, Pa Kua and Five Element theory are the most important of these.

THE SUPREME POLARITIES (TAI CHI)

The term Tai Chi has been used as early as in both Chuang Tzu's textual work and the *Oracle Book of I-Ching* (or *I-Jing*, meaning the *Book of Changes*). Ancient Taoists epitomized Tao graphically in a simplistic Tai Chi symbol. Tai Chi literally means the great extremities or the supreme polarities. It is made up of two polar halves engulfed within a circle, symbolizing its bipolar unity and the eternal nature of cyclonic transformations. The Yang pole represents the male, the light, the warm and the active natures of the polar force, while the Yin pole represents the female, the dark, the cold and the subdued natures of the polar force. Both polarities are interlocking and mirroring each other with a wavy shape. Each polarity contains a small proportion of the opposing polar force in a small circle symbolizing its generative nature. When the polar force is at its full potential, it will give birth to the opposing polar force. If you spin the Tai Chi symbol round on its central axis, you can see the pattern of continuous fusion as the polarities flow into each other. The interplay and the fusion of Yin and Yang is the dynamic continuum of causality – the cosmic mechanics of creation and destruction.

Taoists believe that the balance of Yin and Yang factors is the foundation of harmony of all things in the universe. If man follows the same principles, harmony can be achieved in all human situations. In Chinese medicine, the Yin and Yang concept plays a vital role in balancing and healing. For example, if a person suffers from constipation, it is due to excessive heat (Yang) in the colon. Drinking a cool (Yin) herbal tea will calm down the heat and reclaim the fluid balance of the body. The Tai Chi symbol thus represents the cyclical balance of polarities, the self-harmonizing, the ever-transforming, the ever-integrating and the ever-procreating oneness.

陰

陽

Tao gives birth to one. One gives birth to two. Two gives birth to three and three gives birth to the myriad things. When the myriad things are filled with the energy of Yin and Yang, it is in a state of harmony.

TAO TE JING

THE FIVE ELEMENTS (WU XING)

Further to the Yin and Yang principle, Taoists observed nature and discovered the dynamic principle of the mutual generating and the mutual subjugating forces of the Five Elements. The Five Elements, metal, wood, water, fire and earth, are the archetypal representations of these balancing forces. Nature maintains its balance by the continuous interplay of mutual generation (nourishing) and subjugation (destroying) of all the Five Elements (see page 14).

The generative relationships are as follows:

• wood produces fire
• fire creates earth
• earth yields metal
• metal makes water
• water supplies wood

The subjugative relationships are as follows:
• wood subjugates earth
• earth overcomes water
• water quenches fire
• fire tames metal
• metal overpowers wood

When the relationships of the mutual generation and subjugation of the elements apply to nature and human bodies, harmonious control can be applied in agriculture, medicine and all human conditions. The Five Element principle is widely used in farming, cooking, medicine, divination of placement (Feng Shui) and martial arts. Some of the world's most renowned dishes from the Chinese cuisine are based on the Five Element principle. Sweet and sour sauce has a generating factor from the earth and wood elements to complement each other's flavour. Hot and sour soup has a subjugating factor of the metal and wood elements to allow the two tangy flavours to stand out individually. In fact, the Five Element principle has embedded itself into the Chinese language without being noticed by ordinary Chinese folk. For example, heat in the colon means constipation, wind and humidity mean rheumatism, and excessive fire in the liver or excessive fire energy (Qi) means bad temper.

KEY
— **Generation**
— **Subjugation**

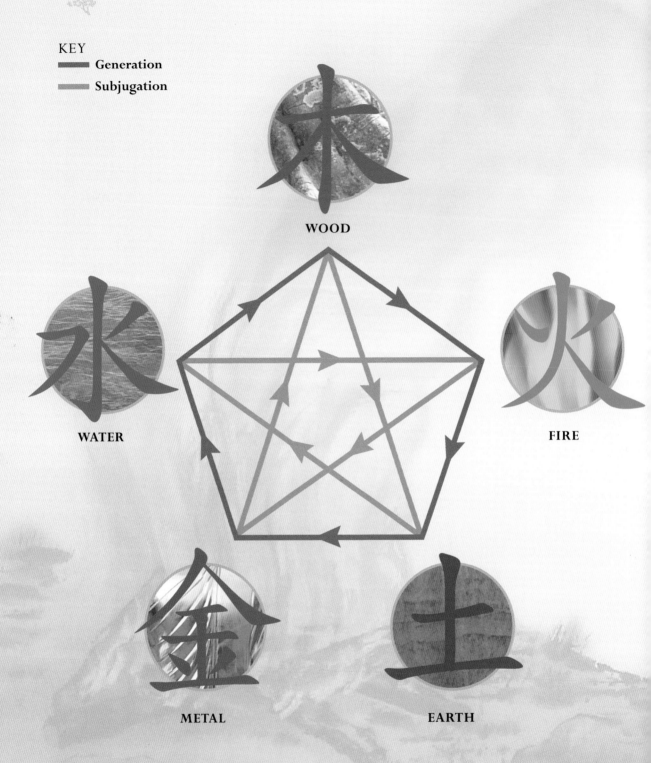

WOOD

WATER

FIRE

METAL

EARTH

THE FIVE ELEMENTS AND NATURE

Correspondence	Wood	Fire	Earth	Metal	Water
Location	East	South	Centre	West	North
Colour	Green	Red	Yellow	White	Black
Flavour	Sour	Bitter	Sweet	Hot	Salty
Season	Spring	Summer	Mid-summer	Autumn	Winter
Life cycle	Birth	Growth	Maturity	Gathering	Storage
Climate	Wind	Heat	Humidity	Dryness	Chill
Grain	Wheat	Millet	Rye	Rice	Beans
Meat	Chicken	Mutton	Beef	Horse	Pork
Musical note	Mi (Jue)	Soh (Zhi)	Doh (Gong)	Re (Shang)	Lah (Yu)

THE FIVE ELEMENTS AND THE HUMAN BODY

Correspondence	Wood	Fire	Earth	Metal	Water
Yin organ	Liver	Heart	Spleen	Lungs	Kidneys
Yang organ	Gall bladder	Small intestine	Stomach	Large intestine	Bladder
Facial feature	Eyes	Tongue	Mouth	Nose	Ears
Body feature	Tendons	Blood vessels	Muscles	Skin	Bones
Emotion	Anger	Joy	Obsession	Sadness	Fear
Sound	Shout	Laugh	Sing	Wail	Sigh
Fluid	Tears	Sweat	Saliva	Mucus	Urine

THE EIGHT TRIGRAMS (PA KUA)

The Pa Kua symbol also plays a very important role in Taoism. The Pa Kua is made up of eight trigrams situated in the eight directions of 45 degree rotation. A trigram is made up of three lines. These lines can be continuous of Yang nature or broken of Yin nature. When two trigrams combine, they form a hexagram. There are altogether 64 combinations of hexagrams, which are the archetypal representations of all things, all events and all situations in the universe and they are used for divination of oracles in the *Book of Changes (I-Ching)*.

I-Ching was formulated specially to interpret the hexagrams. Each of the 64 hexagrams in the *I-Ching* contains a name, a judgement and its commentary. Legend told that a mystical person Fu Hsi (2852–2738 BCE) discovered the secrets of nature of the eight trigrams on the side of a dragon. Fu Hsi merged the numerical values of the dragon diagram to formulate the Hé Tú or River Map. Then King Wen in about 600 BCE developed an idea of combining all possible combinations of the trigram pairs to produce the 64 hexagrams of the *I-Ching* and assigned a name to each one. He also wrote the core interpretation for each hexagram called the Judgements. The Duke of Chou later wrote the further commentary on individual lines and what the symbolism involved. Subsequently, Confucius (Kung Fu Tzu), a contemporary patriarch ethicist of Chuang Tzu, annotated further commentary known as the Ten Wings.

I-Ching's divination of oracles is not based on any beliefs of fatalism, as Taoists do not believe in fixed destiny. Like all things in the universe, our life is also going through constant transformation. As we are all responsible for our own destinies, it is entirely up to each one of us to shape our own life and create our own future. Consulting the *I-Ching* does not miraculously provide a definitive solution to a particular situation, but it can inspire someone with certain directions and creative alternatives so that they are able to deal with the situation more harmoniously.

The Pa Kua is an archetypal representation of harmony. This means harmony within oneself and harmony with the environment (nature). During the first two stages of the Heaven Primal Elixir Meditation, the Microcosmic Cycle (Xiao Zhou Tien) of Qi rotation passes through eight main Chinese chakra points (Three Gateways, Three Dan Tiens, Crown Point and Perineum Point. These psychic centres are not the same as the ones in the Hindu tradition, although some of them may be in similar locations.) We can loosely call them the Pa Kua points because of the eight directional positions of the circle, but one should not look too deeply into the archetypal meanings or search for any parallel intellectual meanings from the *I-Ching*. The Heavenly Primal Elixir Meditation is also called the Kan Li Meditation because it involves the process of fusion between the kidney energy and the heart energy, which is symbolized by water (Kan) and fire (Li) respectively in the Pa Kua.

The Great Masters

Although the precise origin of Taoism is unknown, it is however widely accepted by contemporary scholars and clerics alike that Lao Tzu was the grand master of Taoism and the Yellow Emperor was the most prominent traceable source of the Immortal tradition.

Taoist mysticism is often known as the 'Haung Lao thoughts' in honouring the two great masters. Chuang Tzu is regarded as the third most important master due to his profound insight at the humanistic, philosophical and scholastic levels.

THE YELLOW EMPEROR

The Yellow Emperor (Haung Di) is believed to be the first Emperor of the unified China after he defeated the Yan Emperor and unified China as one nation. Most Chinese today consider him to be the common ancestor of all Chinese people because of his vast contributions to their civilization. Scholars conferred the name Yellow Emperor on him in honour of his immense cultural and technological input. The colour yellow was bestowed on him for sentimental reasons, because it is the colour of the earth element and agriculture has always been an important occupation in China. The Yellow Emperor's achievements are linked to the earth, a cultural cradle for nourishment and growth. During his reign, the Yellow Emperor together with his imperial ministers created new systems and new inventions, which shaped China as a new moralistic civilization. Their contributions included Chinese writing, coins, boats, carts, compasses, musical notes, a lunar calendar, mathematics, silk weaving, military strategy,

weapons and the medical books *Internal Book* (*Nei Jing*) and Short Questions (*Su Wen*).

It is impossible to prove or disprove whether all of these contributions were made during the Yellow Emperor's reign. Imperial historians tended to over-exaggerate their Emperor's achievements for one reason or another. Some of the subsequent Alchemists even borrowed the

Yellow Emperor's name as the author of their textual work. Despite that, his medical books *Nei Jing* and *Su Wen* have been regarded as the most influential contribution to Chinese Taoist culture. It is widely believed that the Yellow Emperor and his ministers practised the Alchemy Meditation to gain longevity and Immortality. Their early meditation practices involved very simplistic methods such as 'quietude of the mind (Xin Zhai)' and 'sitting still and detaching from thought (Zuo Wang)'. These simplistic approaches may have been silent influences on the Zen Meditation tradition subsequently.

The unbiased purity of mind in Xin Zhai is paralleled to Christ's proclamation of 'Blessed are the pure in heart, for they shall see their God.' This purity of mind can also be found synonymously in Buddhism. Avalokitesvara Boddhisattva was once instructed by his guru to practise the meditation concerned with hearing. 'At the beginning, I was listening into the stream

with my ears. My ears became detached. When I detached from the sound and the stream, there was no more stillness and chaos. When I advanced further, all things disappeared. When I realized the non-existence of all things, all things were embraced by the void. Then, both creation and annihilation disappeared with the manifestation of nirvana.'

Zuo Wang on the other hand is the meditation of letting go of one's ego. Selflessness and humility are the direct self-cultivating qualities from Zuo Wang. The illusory nature of all things was not directly deduced as it is in Buddhism but, in its very subtle way, the Taoist's view of the material world is actually very similar to the Maya (great illusion) concept. Taoists do not, however, consciously and objectively reject or confirm materialism. Instead, by understanding the dualistic nature of the perpetual transformation of all things, Taoists adopt the middle way of non-attachment to both gain and loss.

Something evolved from the chaos before the formation of the universe. It is inaudible and inconceivable. It is omnipotent and immutable. It is omnipresent and eternal. It may be regarded as the mother of the universe.

TAO TE JING

LAO TZU (OLD MASTER)

Lao Tzu was a keeper of the Imperial Archives in the Royal Palace Library during the warring Chou Dynasty (1121–249 BCE). Lao Tzu resigned his post and hopped on a buffalo to go off to retire for the rest of his life in the mountains. When he arrived at the Castle Gate (Han Gǔ Guan), the official in charge, Yin Xi, requested that Lao Tzu write a book on Tao for him. Lao Tzu wrote down his mystical insight about Tao and its implementation in some 5,000 words called *Tao Te Jing*. He then went westward and lived a very simple hermitic life, meditating among the high mountains and the clouds, and lived to the exceptional old age of 180.

Tao Te Jing is one of the most frequently translated and widely read books in the world. *Tao Te Jing* is a book of cosmological, philosophical and mystical wisdom. Lao Tzu could have been the first man on earth more than 2,500 years ago to conceive that the universe was born out of chaos. This idea is totally paralleled and consistent with modern scientific observation today.

Through meditation, Lao Tzu understood the greatness of Tao. He knew its virtues of flexibility, ever becoming and ever transforming, its spontaneity, its adaptation to changes, its ability to contain and to dispose and to act without displaying.

If man can learn from these virtues, he can attain great harmony in his life. Man should therefore take his lesson from observing the earth. The earth should take its lesson from the way of heaven. Heaven should take its lesson from Tao as Tao takes its lesson from spontaneity. The spontaneity comes from the ability of non-action (Wu Wei).

The Taoist doctrine of non-action (Wu Wei) is the principle of following the way of nature and withdrawing from taking any impulsive actions. If we follow the natural drive, the natural rhythm and natural transformation, all things will be done according to their own nature or way and at their own time. The decision of taking the non-action path must not be viewed as a fatalistic view of surrendering our lives to all eventualities. It is a conscious and intelligent decision to harmonize with nature and within our very selves. Therefore, the pursuit of selflessness and the practice of meditation are also conscious and intelligent decisions. By adopting non-action introspectively,

The softest in the world can overcome the hardest. It came from nowhere and yet it can penetrate everywhere, I thence understand the advantage of non-action (Wu Wei). Only a few (people) in the world have mastered the teaching of quietude and the advantage of Wu Wei.

Without leaving the house,
One knows all about the whole world.
Without looking through the window,
One sees Tao of Heaven.

The further one travels,
The less one knows.
Thus, the sage knows without travelling,
Understands without looking,
Accomplishes without action.

TAO TE JING

The sage conducts his life with Wu Wei and
he practises the doctrine of contemplation.
He acts without lordship.
He lives without ownership.
He gives without wishing for return.
He succeeds without claiming for self-importance.
Because he does not claim for self-importance,
he is always regarded as important.

Those who are acting (with lordship) will certainly fail.
Those who are holding on (ownership) will certainly lose.
The Sage abides by Wu Wei, that he will never fail.
He does not hold on, that he will never lose.

TAO TE JING

we can unveil the preconceived rationality, emotions and beliefs so as to perceive the true nature of reality.

The word 'travelling' in *Tao Te Jing* refers to rational knowledge, the indoctrinated perception that one acquires from one's own educational, cultural and social environments. On the humanistic level, Wu Wei requires people to have fewer desires and fewer expectations in life. If one pursues life with and for simplicity, moderation, compassion and humility, one will never be without. Nature will find its own way to compensate its shortcomings and its insufficiency. If, on the other hand, people act upon their own ambition, self-importance and self-interests, they will bring about disaster as a result of their own actions.

Lao Tzu saw the dynamic interplay of Yin and Yang as one. On the ethical level, we must understand the oneness of the polarities and we must not fix onto either extreme. This understanding formulates the Taoist thinking behind taking the middle way in all actions. When we take the middle way, we learn to become moderate and selfless.

When the world regards something as
beautiful, then ugliness will appear. When
the world regards something as righteous,
then evil will appear.

To be imperfect and you will become perfect.
To be bent and you will become straight.
To be empty and you will become filled.
To be worn and you will become refurbished.

TAO TE JING

CHUANG TZU OR MASTER CHUANG

Chuang Tzu (369–286 BCE) was a follower of Lao Tzu's tradition and a contemporary patriarch of the ethicist Confucius and politician Mo Tzu. After quitting his well-paid official job he decided to live a simple, hermitic life and devote his whole life to meditation in order to become an Immortal. Chuang Tzu is considered to be the second most influential Taoist philosophical thinker after master Lao Tzu. While Lao Tzu's teaching concentrated on the philosophical,

Those who dream of drinking wine merrily may wake to lamentation and sorrow. Those who dream of lamentation and sorrow may wake to enjoy the hunt. While they are dreaming, they do not know that they are dreaming and they may even interpret the very dream they are dreaming about. It is only when they are awakened, they then realize they have been dreaming. And only then comes the greatest awakening when we realize that this life is really a great dream.

BOOK OF CHUANG TZU, CHAPTER 2

cosmological and mystical aspects of Tao, Chuang Tzu on the contrary was a humorous storyteller and an optimistic psychoanalyst. He used parables, stories and paradox to illustrate his teaching. His teaching is crystallized in a 33-chapter *Book of Chuang Tzu*. At the core of his teaching is the belief that man can only achieve true liberation and true happiness if he understands Tao and lives in harmony with all things.

Chuang Tzu looked deep into the human psyche and he recognized the dualistic interplay and the homogeneity of dreams and the wakened consciousness. Chuang Tzu understood the illusion

I, Chuang Chou, once dreamed that I was a butterfly that I was happily and freely flitting around. I was not conscious that I was Chuang Chou. Suddenly, I woke up and there again Chuang Chou I was. I don't know whether Chuang Chou was dreaming that he was a butterfly or the butterfly was dreaming that it was Chuang Chou. This is called transformation of matters.

BOOK OF CHUANG TZU, CHAPTER 3

of reality and our inability to hold onto life and material belongings. Therefore, he taught us to conduct a totally carefree and worry-free outlook.

Chuang Tzu said, 'A supreme man is selfless while a spiritual man does not claim for honour and a sage disregards self-importance.' Chuang Tzu believed that an ideal society is a society where people attain the virtue of selflessness. He understood the constant transformation of all things and that man can only be truly liberated if he allows the letting go of himself (ego) from all bondage. Good or bad, rich or poor, loss or gain, life or death are all momentary and ever transforming because this is that and that is this or this can be transformed into that and vice versa. It is consequently pointless to compare one to the other. As nothing is absolute or eternal in life or in death, man must learn to accept without prejudice and detach himself from all things.

When Chuang Tzu's wife died, he sat on a mat singing and beating a drum instead of mourning for her death. He explained to his friend Hui Shih, who was angry at his actions. Chuang Tzu answered thus:

'No, if this was her initial death, how could I not be saddened? However, let us observe her from the beginning. Originally, there was no birth and formless. There was no Qi either. Out of the vast chaos, a transformation occurred and there was Qi. Qi transformed into form and form transformed into lives. And now, it transforms again into death. This is similar to the rotation of the four seasons. My wife is now sleeping in a large palace (referring to Tao). If I were to mourn her with crying, I would be ignorant of the meaning of life. This is the reason why I stop myself from mourning.'

(Book of Chuang Tzu, Chapter 18)

Immortality and the Alchemy Meditation

Taoist esoteric techniques for promoting Qi harmonization and spiritual liberation are generally known as Immortalism (Xian Shu). Early Taoism was purely a philosophical and mystical pursuit. Contemplation was a means of self-cultivation and harmonization with one's natural environment and the universe.

Early Taoist meditation techniques were widely developed and practised by poets, artists, hermits and sages. As these early fragmentary techniques went through the process of gradual refinement, they laid down the foundations for the subsequent Alchemy Meditation techniques for Immortalism.

Similar to the Hindu and the Buddhist meditation traditions of liberating sentient beings from the karmic cycle (the teaching that all our actions have consequences on our future actions), Taoists of China also have perfected the esoteric techniques of Alchemy Meditation to liberate the Spirit (Shen) from the cycle of birth and reincarnation. The Taoist pathway of spiritual enlightenment involves restoration and refinement of all physical, psychical and spiritual energies. The transformation of these energies rejuvenates the physical body and extends the life span. An enlightened Spirit becomes selfless and gradually levitates out of the body to unify with Tao, the source of all creation and the great void. The enlightened Spirit will thus become an Immortal. Fundamentally, such practice is aimed at re-establishing the psycho-cosmic kinship between our high consciousness (Spirit) and our creator (Tao).

Early Taoists are called Tao Jia and Xian Jia (Immortals). Fundamentally, there were no significant differences between Tao Jia and Xian Jia as they both adopted the same living principles of following Tao. Xian Jia, however, dedicated their entire lives to achieve Immortality and they lived as hermits with very little or no engagement with the society at large. It is generally believed that the Immortalists may have originated during the Warring States Period (475–221 BCE) in the coastal areas of the Yan and Qi States. The early Immortalists were described as the Authentic Men (Zhen Ren), the Formula Masters (Fang Shi) and the Immortal Men (Xian Ren). The Authentic Men were equivalent to the wise men or sages in western traditions. The Formula Masters were magicians or medicine men, and the Immortal Men were highly evolved spiritual beings with divine attributes.

The Taoists believe that all things come from the same self-generative and procreative universal source of Tao. Tao creates the universal primal energy (Yuen Qi). Qi is the universal energy, which permeates all things in the universe. Qi is the reservoir of life, which circulates round the meridian network of our body. According to the Yellow Emperor's *Internal Book* (*Nei Jing*), there are different types of Qi within the human body, such as nutritional Qi (Jan Qi), Defender Qi (Wai Qi) and Respiratory Qi (Chung Qi). All of them come from the same source of Universal Primal Qi (Yuen Qi). Universal Primal Qi occurs during the chaos before the birth of the universe.

The word 'one' (see quotation above right) refers to the Universal Primal Qi. This is the energy that gave birth to the universe and myriad things. We were all born with different levels of Primal Qi

Tao gave birth to one.
One gave birth to two.
Two gave birth to three.
Three gave birth to myriad things.

TAO TE JING

and Essence of Life (Jing) in our body. Our kidneys are responsible for storing and regulating the emissions of Jing energy. Jing governs our growth, health, virility and vitality throughout our whole life. The level of Jing in our body is manifest in both our physical and mental wellbeing. The degeneration of kidney functions and the low level of Jing emission directly affect fears, worries, illnesses and old age. As we age, Jing will become scarce, and when Jing is exhausted our physical body will die. By practising the Alchemy Meditation, one can transform the Jing energy into the refined Universal Primal Qi. The transformation of this energy creates a psychosomatic harmonization, which will promote emotional equilibrium, good health and longevity.

The sequential transformation of energies involves symbolic processes of medicine collection and medicine formation. For this reason the Alchemy Meditation is generally known as the Internal Elixir Method (Nai Dan Fa). Symbolically, your Lower Dan Tien is treated as a cauldron where the physical, psychical and spiritual ingredients are gathered, treated and transformed into medicine (elixir). The medicine will gradually nourish your physical, psychical and spiritual spheres and transform them into higher energies and higher inspirations. Once the medicine is mature, your body will be nourished and rejuvenated. Your Spirit (Shen) will be heightened, refined and restored to become pure without expectations, desires and artificiality. It will then be free from the gravitational pull of physical, emotional and material desires.

The Taoist Alchemy Meditation involves four key stages of energy transformation. The psychosomatic harmonization process takes place during the first two stages,

commonly known as 'the restoration of Human Nature (Xing) and Life (Ming)'. Fundamentally, it is the balancing of the heart (fire) and kidney (water) energies. In other words, psychosomatic harmonization is the creation of a healthy body and a healthy mind. Taoist Immortality is a result of the spiritual rebirth involving the transformation of attitudes, energies, perceptions and life orientation.

Taoists perceive being kind to others as being kind to oneself and one's body. When you express kindness, you also generate

harmony, calmness, love, understanding and compassion. These harmonious emotions will resonate happy vibrations within your body creating balance and smooth Qi flow. On the other hand, if you express hatred, greed, jealousy, fear, worry, depression or anger, you will create disharmony within your body, torment your mind and deflate your spirit. Disharmony and imbalanced Qi flow will cause chaos, accelerating ageing and manifesting disease within your body.

THE IMMORTALS

According to the Immortalist tradition, there are five ranks of Immortals, as follows.

- **Ghost Immortals (Gui Xian)** are those who started practising the Alchemy Meditation at an advanced age. Despite their spiritual advancement, their worn and aged body impedes them from physical rejuvenation. Ghost Immortals can achieve their final unification with Tao in their next incarnations via rebirth, or by borrowing a body from a younger person who has just passed over.

- **Human Immortals (Ren Xian)** are those who have accomplished physical rejuvenation and have the ability to enjoy an exceptionally long life. However, they have not yet quite reached the final two stages of the Alchemy Meditation. Although physically they are more advanced than the Ghost Immortals, spiritually they are not as advanced or as liberated as the Ghost Immortals or the Earth Immortals.

- **Earth Immortals (Di Xian)** are those who have perfected the second stage of the meditation. However, their spirit is not yet fully liberated as they are still dwelling in the formative stages of the third part of the meditation. They can only be earth-bound Immortals with exceptional health and longevity.

- **Spirit Immortals (Shen Xian)** are those who have liberated their spirit from their physical body but they are still at the first phase of the final stage of the meditation. They have achieved the perfection of rejuvenating their physical body. They possess heightened psychic abilities enabling them to perceive beyond their normal senses, to enter people's dreams to communicate and to heal with their thoughts. They also have the ability to command their own life and death. The Spirit Immortals are very similar to guardian angels in Christianity or spiritual guides in Spiritualism.

- **Celestial Immortals (Tien Xian)** are the highest rank of Immortals as they have achieved the final stage of the Alchemy Meditation which means unification with Tao. They are endowed with divine attributes so that they can be materialized in multiple dimensions simultaneously. Celestial Immortals are often called Golden Immortals (Jin Xian) because their aura shines with a golden light. They are omnipresent, omnipotent and omniscient as they are the imprinted manifestation of their procreator, Tao. Such transformation of consciousness can only be described as synonymous to Buddhahood in Buddhism or Christ's proclamation of 'I and my Father are one'.

THE
Immortality
PROGRAMME

PREPARATION

Compose and calm your mind and relax your body. This preparatory stage is the first phase of the Taoist Alchemy Meditation. The Heavenly Primal Elixir Meditation requires sharp clarity of internalization and deep, concentrated focus. In order to attune your awareness to a lucid internal reality, you need to learn to calm your mind and to relax your body first.

The preparatory phase is doing just that. When you can still your mind and relax your body then you will be ready to go into the deeper concentration procedures of the Microcosmic Cycle of Qi described later (see pages 70–73). It is not uncommon that most people do not know how to relax their bodies and minds. During our wakened consciousness our senses are continuously receiving and processing signals and information from our external world whether we are aware of them consciously, subconsciously or unconsciously. As a survival instinct, our mind is constantly calculating, responding and then commanding our physical and mental reactions in response to the information collected by our senses from our external environments. Therefore, in our wakened consciousness, our focus of thought is constantly active in dealing with many facets of the external environment. While our senses are continuously in operation, our bodies are also continuously reacting to their demands as well. One of such responses is the 'fight or flight response'.

FIGHT OR FLIGHT

The fight or flight response is an evolutionary survival instinct in the event of an emergency. When you are confronted with a dangerous situation, the hypothalamus in your brain sends out a signal to your adrenal glands and, within seconds, the surging of the survival hormone adrenaline enables you to run faster, hit harder, yell louder, hear and see more sharply than you normally could. Your heart rate is now pumping at twice its normal speed to release reserved energy to all the major muscles in your arms and legs. All other major functions of your body, such as digestion and reproduction, temporarily shut down in order to give you a better chance of survival. This 'fight or flight response' is most invaluable when we are confronted with life-threatening dangers that may jeopardize our physical survival.

Today, most of the dangers we have to confront are not life-threatening situations but our evolutionary instinct is still continuously

responding as if it is. Whether it is a trivial row with your spouse, or someone tooting the horn at you in a traffic jam, or negotiating for a tough contract in your working environment, or looking for your misplaced document before an important business meeting, your natural instinct will immediatey interpret it as a critical situation. Your body is thus constantly reacting to these situations as real mortal dangers, and secretes adrenaline in order to prepare you for your struggle to survive.

However, as a modern person, you are also expected to act with a degree of civility, and somehow, you will act calmly by constraining your emotions and your physical reactions, even when your survival instinct is urging you to run or to fight. This long-term bombardment of adrenaline saturation and your body's inability to dispose of the hormone will eventually manifest adverse effects such as stress, rage, depression, fatigue, anxiety, stomach ulcers, high blood pressure or heart disease. Therefore, if you are experiencing symptoms such as frequent headaches, tension in your shoulders and neck, anxiety, uncontrollable anger, inexplicable rashes, giddiness, dizziness, chronic fatigue, hot flushes, indigestion or insomnia, you may be suffering from various forms of stress.

MEDITATION

The meditation exercise (see pages 39–43) will re-educate your body to relax and to over-ride your fight or flight response. It will also re-educate your mind to slow down and to differentiate between what is a life-threatening situation and what is not. You will learn to master the art of deep concentration by withholding your thoughts and blanking your mind from all external distractions. When you are in a state of Deep Relaxation, it will allow your body to reregulate and to heal itself. Once your body learns to be totally relaxed, your concentration will also be heightened. This will allow your mind to attune itself into a pure state of consciousness. Buddhists describe it as 'the uncontaminated mirror'. When your mind is composed, your thoughts will be untroubled by external influences and a new sense of lucidity will emerge. This novel sense of clarity will allow your mind to see deeply and widely beyond your habitual cognition and rationality. It will also enable you to experience a fresh flexibility toward creativity and thought processing as the boundaries of your habitual cognition and rationality are widened. Once you have mastered this first phase of the Immortal Alchemy Meditation, you will be ready to proceed to the second phase, the Heaven Primal Elixir Meditation (see page 64).

Traditionally, 'Sitting still and detaching from thought' (Zuo Wang), 'Observing the light' (Guan Guang) or 'Regulating the breaths' (Tiao Xi) is practised as the entry meditation induction exercise. However, the way these over-simplistic methods are handled may present tremendous understanding difficulties for the western uninitiated minds. Hence, I have devised an easier approach, which involves a systematic induction sequence. This method can be described as a combination of visualization and 'Observing the light' (Guan Guang).

SMILING

When I was a student of Tai Chi Chuan some 33 years ago, I was taught to wear a slight smile on my face when performing the Tai Chi movements, especially when performing double pushing hands. At the time I did not appreciate the significance of such tiny gestures although I followed the instruction without questioning. I subsequently discovered that smiling is the best and most powerful meditation induction technique for both voluntary and involuntary muscular relaxation. (I have explored the importance of smiling on pages 134–135.)

About 95 per cent of our emotions are expressed from the neck to the top of the head. When you are happy, sad, angry or sympathetic, you will always express these emotions with your facial expressions. If you are greeting someone with a smile or a frown, you will find that they involuntarily mirror your emotions. Researchers in Sweden found that our unconscious minds exert direct control of our facial muscles. Now try this experiment: frown for a few seconds and try to change it to a smile again. You will find it hard to mobilize your facial muscles to perform a real smile afterwards. Instead, you will find yourself struggling to control your facial muscles, so much so that you will end up performing a sad smile no matter how hard you try to smile properly. Now, try to relax the tensed facial muscles by massaging your face for a minute or so. Once the tension is gone, wear a gentle smile on your face again. How does it feel? This time you should feel an easy and happy smile on your face as your facial muscles are relaxed.

The Meditation Environment

It is vital to observe certain simple practices when you meditate, such as choosing a particular time and place and wearing loose-fitting clothes.

THE TIME AND THE PLACE

Select a time of the day to suit your daily routine and reserve this as a dedicated period for your personal privacy. It is advisable to perform your meditation routines at the same place and the same time on a daily basis. Once you have signed up for this spiritual quest, you need to be totally committed if you want to yield results. You need to treat the place for your meditation as a sacred sanctuary and you have to be totally loyal to the allocated time, chosen as the 'golden period' of the day. Don't select a time too close to a vigorous daily routine, on too full a stomach or when your mind is too active with your thoughts after a hard negotiating session at work. Give yourself a period to wind down first, before practising your meditation routines.

If you are going to meditate in a communal area of your house, such as the sitting room, choose a sensible period (such as after all the family members have gone to bed or first thing in the morning before they get up), so that you will not be disturbed. If it is permitted, allocate a room entirely for your meditation activities. If you are working shift duties with varying time rotations, allocate the time with some degree of normality, such as two hours before you go to bed or half an hour after getting up. In such a way, psychologically, you are telling yourself there is a pattern of routine that you are adhering to despite the different shift rotations. Do not choose a time that is too near to your bedtime because you may feel too tired and fall asleep while meditating. Do not meditate as soon as you have got up from bed either, as your consciousness is not yet fully awakened.

CLOTHES

It is of paramount importance that your clothes are comfortable and loose, especially around the waist and chest areas so as to allow diaphragmatic and ribcage movements. During certain stages of the meditation, male students may experience spontaneous penile erections. It is thus advisable for male students not to wear any tight briefs. (This phenomenon called Shēng Yang. A more detailed description can be found on pages 72–73.) Similarly, it is advisable for female students not to wear a bra.

consciousness. Don't use any incense sticks with pungent fragrances as excessive olfactory stimulation can distract your attention span and concentration. If you meditate in the evening, use a small table lamp with a shade on, if you meditate in the daytime, draw the curtains to reduce bright light. Make sure the room is neither too warm nor too cold, because your body's reaction to extreme temperature can externalize your attention and affect your concentration. Finally, if you meditate in a room, keep the door closed as a gesture that you are temporarily shutting yourself away from the external world, but make sure that the ventilation is adequate.

THE SANCTUARY

Once you have chosen the time and place, you need to make sure that your sanctuary is always clean and tidy. Clear out all the unnecessary clutter, as a sparsely decorated room is more desirable. A simple, clean and tidy environment gives the mind the signals of tranquillity and readiness, while a busy, dirty and cluttered environment bombards the mind with the same kinds of frenetic energy. You can also light a stick of incense or a scented candle to jazz up the atmosphere. Better still, you can use an ionizer or an aromatherapy vaporizer. The ionizer simulates the atmosphere and clean air of high mountains by emitting negative ions, while a vaporizer emits a gentle healing fragrance. Some of the essential aromatic oils such as lavender or pine needle emit a tranquillizing fragrance, which can greatly encourage your mind to attune to a meditative

Posture

There is no fixed posture for meditation. However, it is important that you maintain a good sitting posture, or you will hinder the progress of your meditation.

You can either sit on a chair or sit on the floor. If you sit on the floor, it is preferable to sit on a carpet or a rug. The traditional way of floor sitting is crossing one leg in front of the other. If you prefer, you can also do a single or a double yoga lotus position. If you sit on a chair, spread out your legs squarely and evenly, slightly wider than shoulder width. If you suffer from back trouble, you can put a cushion behind your back to give your back some support. It is of utmost

importance to sit with your back upright without slouching or protruding your abdomen or tilting your shoulders. Bad postures will upset the balance of the body and your concentration. A classical tenet called 'Four Ways of Equilibrium' sums up the importance of the correct meditation posture in three sentences:

When your head is in equilibrium,
 your body will be in equilibrium.
When your body is in equilibrium,
 your energy (Qi) will be in equilibrium.
When your energy is in equilibrium,
 your mind will be in equilibrium.

Once you have sat down in a comfortable and relaxed position of your choice, rub your palms together until they are hot. Put your palms over your face and massage your face with a circular movement 36 times. Sense the muscle tones with the tips of your fingers and concentrate on the tensed muscle areas by applying deeper pressure with your massage. You can perform the massage longer with more repetitions, if you prefer, until you are satisfied with the relaxation of your face. Now put your palms down on your laps and place them into a Tai Chi gesture (Mudra). You are now ready to proceed to the next stage of the meditation.

Traditionally, left is considered to be a male element and right to be a female element. Therefore, a man should put the left palm below the right palm, while a woman should put the right palm below the left palm. This rule also applies to the legs if you are sitting with your legs crossed. Personally speaking, I think such a rule is over-ritualistic and restrictive. The way we place our hands is determined by whether we are left-handed or right-handed and whether it is a habitual gesture. So, as long as you feel comfortable with your palms and legs, it does not really matter about the traditional left and right concept at all.

DEEP RELAXATION

Relaxing deeply is the first part of the Alchemy Meditation. Practising this routine regularly develops the clarity and concentration needed to perform the Alchemy Meditation successfully. You can also use this technique to relieve everyday stress.

You do not need to learn all of the steps of the routine at once. Build up the routine gradually at your own pace. Read the steps below several times to learn the sequence. Practise the routine daily for 15–30 minutes, and you may experience a gradual transformation of your whole being. For instance:

- You may feel more relaxed, calmer and better able to deal with problems

- Your thinking may become more creative so you can reason clearly and make decisions and take action without rushing

- You may feel more energetic and require less sleep

- You may see and hear with more clarity, and your field of perception may widen

Practise this routine daily until you experience positive evidence of transformation, of deep physical relaxation and a sense of lasting tranquillity. Then you will be ready to go on to the next stage of the Alchemy Meditation while enjoying life as a much happier, relaxed and positive person inside your own soul.

Step 1

- Swallow any excess saliva in your mouth with one gulp and curl your tongue up, gently touching the roof of your mouth.

- Close your eyes and allow your facial muscles to relax into a happy smile.

- Breathe gently, slowly and naturally, but prolong and deepen your breaths using diaphragmatic movements. Don't force anything unnatural.

Deep diaphragmatic breathing will occur automatically once your body is totally relaxed. The more you relax, the deeper your breathing will become.

- Now sense your facial relaxation and the joyous emotion that is brought about by your smile. The happier you feel inside, the more your face and forehead will relax.

Step 2

- Expand the sensation of relaxation and happiness throughout your head, including your forehead at the front, the temporal areas at the sides, the crown at the top, and the occipital area at the back of your head.

- Retain these sensations and absorb them into your consciousness for a minute or two.

- Allow these sensations to become a joyous radiance emanating outward.

- Bathe in this warm radiance for a blessed moment and see all of your worries, anger and anxiety dissolved by this radiance, like melting butter dripping down from your head.

Step 3

- Take a moment to enjoy this wonderful sensation of relaxation and allow your consciousness to recognize the emancipation from your old, tense self.

- In your own time, allow this joyous radiance to migrate down towards your neck.

- Recognize the habitual tension you have built up in your neck and allow the radiance to dissolve the tension like melting butter.

- As the tension dissolves, sense your head held higher and higher. As your head is held higher, feel a new sense of positive inspiration and confidence emanating from your posture.

Step 4

- Direct the radiance down onto your shoulders.

- Recognize the tension in your shoulders that makes you negative, angry, worried, impulsive and aggressive.

- Allow the radiance to expel all the negativity by dissolving the tension in your muscles and tendons, and deep into your collarbones.

- Let the warmth and joy penetrate into your inner being to console and strengthen your will, as your troubles, your negativity, your anger, your anxiety, your impulsiveness and your aggression melt away.

Step 5

- Feel the radiance massaging downward into your thoracic area, both at the front and at the back of your body.

- Recognize the tension in your chest and allow it to melt away so that your ribcage can stretch outward and open.

- Extend the flow of radiance downward along your arms as far as the tips of your fingers.

- Recognize the tension in your arms and allow the radiance to melt it away so that you will no longer be impulsive or rush into actions.

- Let the melting sensation glide further down toward your abdomen and lower back.

- Recognize the habitual tension that causes backaches and stomach cramps.

- Allow the radiance to penetrate deep into your muscles and spine.

- Sense the joyous emancipation of the dissolving of tension in your muscles and spine. Experience the sense of inner strength and courage as your upper body stretches longer and longer.

Step 6

- Let the radiance move down onto your hip and buttock areas. See the radiance flowing downward extending toward your legs as far as to the tips of your toes.

- Recognize the tension that made you want to run and to escape. Allow the radiance to pacify the deep anxiety within and to slow down the impulsiveness within the muscles.

- When your whole external body is filled with this joyous radiance, feel the deep relaxation and blissful sensation that has been brought about in all your muscles, tendons and ligaments.

- Absorb and enjoy the full body massage from the radiance of your smile for a few minutes and allow the whole body to smile with you.

Step 7

- Now shine this radiance inward into your body and feel the warmth enter your lungs, your heart, stomach, liver, spleen, pancreas, kidneys, intestines and bladder, and to permeate inside all your blood vessels.

- Allow your whole being to experience and to absorb this glorious glow, the joyous warmth and the deep relaxation within for a few minutes.

Step 8

• In your own time, concentrate the radiance onto the midpoint between your eyebrows, the Upper Dan Tien (Yin Tang) area, often known as the third eye. Without using any elaborate effort, put all your focus onto this location and see the radiance as a round bright glow.

• Allow yourself to be totally absorbed into the glow and let go of all your thoughts while retaining the sensation of deep relaxation from your smile.

• Put all your concentration totally onto the glow and slowly let go of all external and internal thoughts including the routines you have just performed.

• Your mind will gradually transform itself into a new state of clarity where there is no thought, no expectation, no judgement and no duality, but pure reflection of suchness, being, existence and profound understanding.

Step 9

• Don't rush yourself when coming out of your meditation. You don't need to time the duration of the process, either as your mind will tell you when to stop.

• When you come out of your meditative consciousness, make it gradual and gentle. Be composed for a moment or two before opening your eyes slowly.

• You can now do the complementary exercises as described in the next chapter to finish off your routines.

Common Questions

Q **Could I practise the Heaven Primal Elixir Meditation (Tien Yuen Dan Fa) without practising the preparatory meditation first?**

If you have previously practised Qi Gong or yoga and if you really understand how to attune your body and mind to a meditative state, you can certainly skip the preparatory phase. However, it is always good practice to follow through all the procedures, as you can only gain more from the experience and you may learn something new from it.

Q **What is the purpose of curling up my tongue to touch the roof of my mouth?**

The main purpose is to give you another focal point of concentration. Traditionally, there are three tips of concentration. You should look at the tip of the nose with your eyes closed. Then imagine the nose tip is looking at the tip of the tongue and, finally, direct the tip of the tongue to look at your heart. In Chinese medicine the tongue is the outlet of our heart because we use our speech to express our feelings. Thus, fixing the tongue and keeping it motionless also symbolizes keeping the mind still.

Q **What shall I do when my mouth fills with saliva after a while?**

Simply swallow the saliva gently without disturbing your concentration.

Q **When I felt relaxed, my body started to sway and my hands started to tremble. Why?**

This is a natural occurrence, which happens to most novices. Imagine that you have been carrying a heavy package for a while and, when you suddenly unload your package, your hands will start to shake and tremble as your body continuously responds to the memory of the heavy load. Our habitual body tension from the fight and flight responses mirrors the effects of lifting or carrying a heavy package. When we suddenly let go of the package (tension) through meditation, our bodies will require a period to accustom to a new burden-free body.

Q **I found it very hard to make my breaths deeper and longer. Did I do anything wrong? How could I amend the problem?**

The problem of shallow breaths is caused by the tension of your body and your inability to relax. Don't make any conscious effort to prolong your breaths or force unnatural diaphragmatic movements. Unnatural breathing can cause adverse effects on your lungs and your heart. Excessive intake of oxygen (hyperventilation) or insufficient intake of oxygen (hypoventilation) can both cause physical harm and create hallucinations to distract your progress. If you feel dizziness or tingling of the fingers and toes, chest pain, or if you see unusual visions, you must stop your meditation at once. You should only breathe naturally and gently through your nose.

Q **Why is it not important to sit in a lotus position?**

Unless you are a student of yoga or you have practised Buddhist meditation for a long time, the lotus position is not the best sitting posture for you. An uncomfortable or painful sitting posture can only cause distraction and upset your concentration. The ancients used to sit with their legs naturally crossed.

Q **When I saw the radiance I got very excited, and as soon as I felt pleased with my progress the radiance disappeared. Why?**

When you let go of your thoughts and your expectations, your concentration will become internalized. If you are excited, your mind builds up bigger expectations of success and your body becomes animated. Your heart will pump faster and your body may also start to twitch from your anticipation. Your mind may become unsettled and impatient and your concentration will be distracted by your excitement.

Q **I could only see pitch black when closing my eyes. Why?**

You were too tense and you closed your eyelids too hard. Try to gently drop down your eyelids without tightening any facial muscles. It is always helpful if you use the smiling sensation as a guideline to relaxation.

COMPLEMENTARY EXERCISES

To inhale and to exhale so as to evacuate the old and replace by the fresh. Imitate the climbing movements of a bear and stretching movements of a bird so as to prolong life.

BOOK OF CHUANG TZU, CHAPTER 15

The precise origin of these exercises has been lost in history. They may have been the predecessors of the famous set Qi Gong exercises 'Eight Pieces of Brocade' and 'Twelve Pieces of Brocade'.

The benefits of complementary exercises are seen in two ways. Firstly, they heighten your body's awareness. The exercises, especially those with the massaging movements, direct your attention to the energy centres and heighten your awareness of muscle tone. They enable you to readjust the muscle condition by flexing, softening and relaxing your body at those areas where you massage them. These exercises also direct your attention toward the body parts that involve energy circulation, which you may not be aware of normally in your wakened consciousness. Secondly, these exercises improve the efficiency of your body's circulation of blood and Qi. They act like kick-starters, mobilizing the Qi movement at the beginning of meditation and give your body a

well-conditioned workout at the end of the meditation session.

Traditionally, apart from the three massaging exercises, dry face wash (Ca Mian), Dan Tien massage (Mo Dan Tien) and back massage (Mo Bei), all other exercises are performed at the end of the meditation section. From my own experience I find that some of these exercises are more beneficial if performed before the meditation, while other exercises are more appropriate after the meditation. However, if you prefer, you can always perform a few exercises at the beginning of the meditation and then perform the rest after the meditation.

Most of these exercises require you to sit down on the floor. Therefore, if you have adopted sitting on a chair as your meditation position, you need to readjust your meditation environment to perform these exercises. There are no straight rules as to how to conduct these routines, but I

would strongly advise novices to follow the full instructions described in this chapter as well as the information in the previous chapter. Most of these exercises do not require any special breathing techniques apart from the double empty lifting exercise (Shuang Kong Ju), which requires inhaling and exhaling to be synchronized with the appropriate movements. Breathe naturally, as you normally would, and don't rush through the exercises, especially the stretching exercises, which require slow movements to maximize the effects.

Traditionally, most individual exercises are repeated 36 times. The main reason for such a practice is due to the phonetic symbolic significance of the number 36. In the Chinese language, phonetically 'three' sounds like 'birth' or 'regeneration' while 'six' sounds like 'continuity', and when they are added together as 'nine' it sounds like 'eternity'. Hence, 36 is a frequently used figure in Chinese culture because of its auspicious symbolic significance for good fortune. It is certainly a substantial number of repetitions for an effective workout; however, it is not a necessary benchmark to adhere to. Therefore, if you prefer, there is no harm at all if you increase or decrease your repetitions for each exercise according to your personal physical capability.

DRY FACE WASH (CA MIAN)

This exercise is sometimes described as 'cat face wash' as it may have taken its inspiration from observing cats washing themselves. This exercise is best performed at the beginning of the meditation because it aids the relaxation of the facial muscles as well as heightening your body's awareness. Other benefits include improvement in the circulation on the facial areas, preventing premature wrinkling and encouraging secretion of natural moisturizing oil, which is essential for a healthy complexion.

- Rub your palms together until they are hot and place them on your face.

- Massage your face in a circular movement from outward to downward to upward and repeat the circle.

- Use your fingers to sense and to detect the textures of your skin and muscle flexibility. Put more pressure on the tense areas where you can sense the tightened muscle tone.

- Try to cover your whole face, including your forehead and chin.

TEETH CLENCHING (KOU CHI)

This exercise is best performed before the meditation, as it will heighten your body's awareness of the facial area as well as the perineum area. The rhythm of squeezing and relaxing could also educate your body to develop awareness and to differentiate between tension and relaxation in these areas.

This exercise stimulates the circulation of your gums and gives the facial muscles around the jaw area a good workout, while the squeezing of the PC muscle (the pubbocoxygennus muscle which is located in the area between your genitals and your anus, often known as the perineum) is a very beneficial exercise for the sexual health of both men and women. Modern medical research confirms that this kind of exercise may tone up and strengthen the muscles of a woman's genitalia, which prevents the prolapse of the uterus at an advanced age. Contemporary medical research from Dr Arnold Kegel discovered that a weak PC muscle could cause weak erections, weak ejaculations, impotence and premature ejaculation in men. This simple exercise promotes blood flow and circulation in your pelvic region and corrects these genitalia problems. It will also help you to develop greater ejaculation control and heighten your body's awareness of your sexual sphere.

- Clench your teeth together hard, without using any force, so that they don't knock together, and hold your bite for nine seconds.

- While you are clenching your teeth, squeeze your perineum or PC muscle and hold the tension for nine seconds, and then relax both your jaw and your PC muscle.

- Don't hold your breath while you are clenching and squeezing but breathe naturally.

- Repeat this exercise another eight times.

STRIKING THE HEAVENLY DRUM (MING TIEN GU)

This traditional Chinese exercise produces a harmonious vibration that massages the inner ears, stimulating your auditory faculty and your brain. It dispels headaches, improves balance and hearing, and improves mental functioning. There are two variations. They are equally effective, especially when practised after the Alchemy Meditation. Choose the variation you prefer or alternate between them.

Heavenly Drum 1

• Rub your palms together until they are hot.

• Place your palms on top of your ears, covering the outer ears, with the fingers placed on the back of the head at the bottom of your skull (occipital area). Cover up your ears well with your palms so that you cannot hear any external noise.

• Gently tap your fingers on the bottom of the skull area with both hands to create a clear 'clong' sound inside your head.

• Tap 36 times in a regular rhythm.

COMPLEMENTARY EXERCISES **51**

Heavenly Drum 2

- Rub your palms together until they are hot.

- Place your palms on top of your ears, covering the outer ears, with the fingers placed on the back of the head embracing the bottom of your skull (occipital area).

- Push both palms forward and backward toward the outer ears three times in a pumping motion.

- Then rest both palms on top of the outer ears to exclude external noise.

- Place the index fingers of each hand on top of the middle fingers and then flick the index fingers simultaneously to hit the muscular areas at the bottom of your skull (occipital area). Your finger motion should create a clear 'clong' sound inside your head. Repeat the flicking movement 36 times in a regular rhythm.

DAN TIEN MASSAGE (MO DAN TIEN)

This exercise is best performed before the meditation to activate the Qi internally. The Lower Dan Tien acts as a cauldron for tempering and storing the transformed energies during the Alchemy Meditation. This exercise will initiate the cauldron and energize the Qi movement for subsequent automation of the Microcosmic Cycle. You can also greatly heighten your body's awareness if you increase the repetitions of the massage by making the Lower Dan Tien centre very hot and more palpable. A revitalized Dan Tien centre will also improve sexual functions.

- Rub your palms together until they are hot.

- Place the right palm on top of the Lower Dan Tien area (7.5 cm/3 in below the navel). Apply firm pressure to massage the location with a clockwise circular movement and repeat the circle 36 times.

- Then place the left palm on top of the Lower Dan Tien area. Apply firm pressure to massage it with an anticlockwise circular movement and repeat the circle another 36 times.

BACK MASSAGE (MO BEI)

This exercise is best performed both before and after the meditation. Performing this exercise before meditation will energize the kidneys and stimulate the emission of Essence of Life (Jing) at the Door of Life centre (Ming Mun) and the kidney areas. Ming Mun is located between the second and the third lumbar vertebrae and it is parallel horizontally to the mid-curve of your waist. Massaging the kidneys is essential for strengthening skeletal health and improves brain functions, virility and vitality. It also helps to heighten the body's awareness of the Ming Mun centre and the kidney areas. This exercise also makes a good warm-up exercise for both double empty lifting (Shuang Kong Ju) and back stretch (Shu Bei).

- Clench your fists and put them on your back over your kidney areas. Use the back of your fists to massage your kidney areas with a circular movement 36 times.

- Ensure that the motion of both fists is in unison. You should feel the muscles getting hotter and hotter on the massaged area.

- You can do more repetitions if you wish, until you get a tingling sensation on the massaged areas.

DOUBLE EMPTY LIFTING (SHUANG KONG JU)

This exercise is best performed after the meditation. This exercise has the effects of lengthening and strengthening your muscles as well as improving the circulation and keeping the joints flexible.

• Stretch your legs out forward while you are in the sitting position. Place both palms on your knees facing upward and interlock the fingers of both palms.

• Then slowly turn them forward and outward and lift them upward with resistance as if you were lifting a heavy boulder. While you are lifting your palms, inhale and synchronize your movement with your breathing. Stretch your palms as high and as far as possible. You should feel your upper body being stretched while you are stretching your arms upward.

• While you are stretching your arms outward or upward, stretch out both legs with your toes pointing upward at the same time with the same rhythm, momentum and resistance. You should stretch them out as far as possible.

• When your palms are fully stretched, bounce them up and down three times and do the similar extra bouncy stretches forward and backward with your legs as well, synchronized with the timing of your arms.

• Then separate your palms and stretch your palms downward, sideward and outward with resistance with a semicircular movement until they are fully stretched. Exhale and make a long 'Hei' sound silently when you are stretching your arms outward. While you are stretching your arms outward or sideward, stretch out both legs with your toes pointing upward at the same time, again using resistance and with the same rhythm and the same momentum. You should stretch out your arms and legs as far as possible.

• When your palms are fully stretched, bounce them backward and forward three times and do the similar extra bouncy stretches backward and forward with your legs simultaneously. You need to synchronize the timing of your arms and your legs.

• Then bring your arms downward from the fully stretched position with a semicircular movement to get your palms back to the first interlocking position on your knees. Keep all your muscles relaxed throughout.

• Pause for a moment or so while breathing naturally to compose yourself.

• Repeat the exercise all over again and do this exercise at least nine times. You can do more repetitions if you wish.

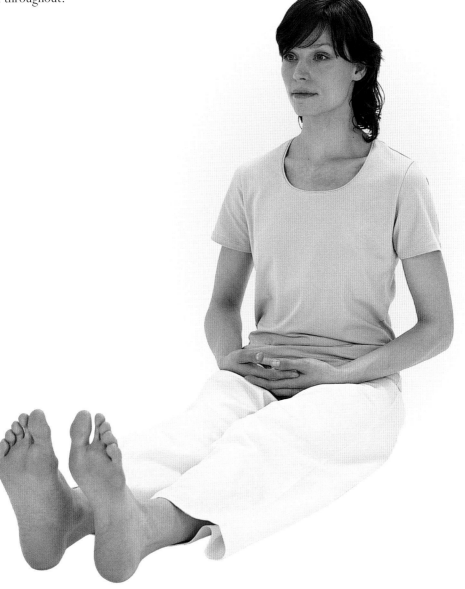

BACK STRETCH (SHU BEI)

This exercise is best performed after the meditation. It will keep your spine supple and has the effect of decompressing the vertebrae. This exercise must not be performed without performing the back massage (Mo Bei) exercise first. It is crucial to perform the back massage (Mo Bei) to warm up the muscles of your back before performing any stretching. If you have not done any stretching exercises before, you must take care to do this exercise slowly; don't be too keen or you might over-stretch your back and injure yourself.

- From the last sitting position, stretch your palms forward and hold onto your feet.

- Bend your head forward and downward toward your knees while keeping your knees straight. You must not bend your knees while stretching forward because you will minimize the effect of this exercise.

- Try to stretch your head forward and downward further each time while you are pulling backward with your palms.

- Repeat this exercise at least nine times.

OOZING SPRING POINT MASSAGE (CA YUNG QUAN)

Massaging this point stimulates the kidney meridian and energizes the kidney Qi. This vital energy improves the strength of your skeletal structure and encourages the regeneration of bones and cartilage. Stimulating the Oozing Spring also helps to improve blood circulation, promote hormonal balance, and revitalize sexual health. The Oozing Spring point is located on the bottom of each foot, on the centre line just behind the sole, between the darker skin and lighter skin.

- Sitting comfortably, gently take hold of your left ankle with your left hand and locate the Oozing Spring point on the bottom of your left foot.

- Using the thumb of your right hand, massage the point in a circular motion.

- After massaging for five minutes, or as long as you wish, reverse your position and massage the Oozing Spring point on the bottom of your right foot with your left thumb.

- If you feel a sharp pain as you massage, you may have energy blockages and a sluggish kidney energy flow. Continuously massaging the Oozing Spring can remove the blockages and reinvigorate the kidney energy.

AXIAL ROTATION (LUN ZHUAN)

This exercise must not be performed without warming up the muscles with back massage (Mo Bei) first. To yield the maximum benefit, it is advisable to perform the back massage (Mo Bei), double empty lifting (Shuang Kong Ju) and back stretch (Shu Bei) first before performing the axial rotation (Lun Zhuan) exercise.

This exercise together with Back stretch (Shu Bei) will strengthen the back muscles and increase the flexibility of your spine. If you hear and feel a click while rotating or stretching your spine, it indicates that a minor displacement of the vertebrae (subluxation) has been repositioned correctly by the torsion. You should feel a sense of relief on the affected area. Most minor back ailments can normally be readjusted by doing these exercises.

- Stand up with your feet 15–22.5 cm (6–9 in) wider than your shoulder width.

- Lift your arms above your shoulders and clench your fists next to your ears as if you were holding a barbell.

- Rotate your waist to the right until the left leg is straight. This is called the Bow and Arrow stance, as one leg is bending like a bow while the other leg is stretching like an arrow. You must hold your arms and fists in the same positions while turning your waist. Try to maximize your rotation without over-doing it and injuring yourself.

- Then rotate your body to the left until the right leg is straight. Once again maintain your arms in the same position while you are rotating your body.

- It is essential to keep your feet firm on the floor with minimum movement while you are rotating your body otherwise, you will reduce the full impact of torsion on your waist.

- Repeat this exercise 36 times.

Common Questions

Q I've read from other sources that Taoist facial massage can be targeted at specific muscles to improve the tonal conditions and the elasticity. Why does the facial massage in this chapter appear to be very basic?

Although dry face wash (Ca Mian) has anti-ageing effects for good complexion, the main function of the facial massage in the complementary exercises is to increase body awareness as well as to relax the muscles to enable a gentle smile. The facial massaging exercises used specifically for improving complexion and muscular tonal conditions are Tuai Na (massage and manipulation) exercises, which require more complex techniques targeting specific muscle groups as well as acupuncture points.

Q Why do I have to rub the palms to make them hot before performing some of the routines?

Firstly, rubbing the palms together can increase your tactility and your body awareness. Secondly, it improves the circulation of blood and Qi by raising the surface temperature.

Q I wear a set of full dentures. Would I still get the benefits from the teeth clenching (Kou Chi) exercise?

Yes, by squeezing and relaxing certain muscles, this exercise can teach you to learn to differentiate the different sensations felt between tension and relaxation. It can also improve the circulation of your gum areas as well as toning up your facial muscles around your jaw area. Most important of all, it can strengthen your PC muscles to improve your sexual health, improve your sexual functions and enhance your sexual enjoyment.

Q I can feel Qi energy swirling at my Lower Dan Tien area after performing the Dan Tien massage (Mo Dan Tien). Is this normal?

Yes, in fact it is a very positive indication of good progress. Most people may feel the Qi energy swirling in circular motions. Some people may even feel the Qi energy swirling in a spherical shape. Any form of Qi movement on the Lower Dan Tien area will enhance the Qi circulation on the central meridians.

Q **How does back massage (Mo Bei) strengthen skeletal health and improve brain functions, virility and vitality?**

In Chinese medicine, kidneys govern the sexual functions, brain functions, skeletal structure and generate bone marrow. They are also the vital organs for storage and emission of Jing energy. Jing is essential for our growth, virility and vitality. Therefore, massaging the kidneys can strengthen the kidney functions as well as enhancing Jing emission. In western medicine, kidneys are organs for fluid and chemical balance as well as eliminating waste products from our blood. Kidneys release EPO hormone, which stimulates the bone marrow to make red blood cells. Insufficient red blood cells will make you feel cold, tired and low in vitality. Kidneys also help your body to use vitamin D, which is essential for strengthening your bones. Therefore, whether you view the body from eastern or western angles, strengthening your kidneys can promote general health, skeletal health, brain functions, virility and vitality.

Q **Since practising the double empty lifting (Shuang Kong Ju) exercise, I notice a marked improvement in my muscular strength. Why?**

Similar to some of the strength-cultivating Qi Gong exercises, double empty lifting (Shuang Kong Ju) employs the same techniques and principles of using the natural body resistance to build up strength.

Q **I am not able to hold onto my feet when performing the back stretch (Shu Bei) exercise and I have difficulty bending my back forward. How can I improve this?**

If you have not previously done any stretching exercises, you might find this exercise very hard and seemingly impossible to perform. Stretch out as much as you can and hold onto your legs as far down as you can until you can finally hold onto your feet. If you increase your bending angle slowly, your muscles will eventually be lengthened enough to enable you to perform this exercise fully.

THE HEAVENLY PRIMAL ELIXIR MEDITATION

Heavenly Primal Elixir Meditation (Tien Yuen Dan Fa) is the ultimate Taoist Alchemy Meditation for rejuvenation, longevity and spiritual enlightenment. Some Taoist Immortals were known to have lived for over three centuries by practising Taoist Alchemy Meditation and adhering to the principles of Tao to live a carefree but non-adulterated lifestyle. The Taoist concept of an extended juvenility, however, is not a conscious vainglorious pursuit but a result of harmonious energy preservation, transformation and restoration.

The Taoist concept of immortality must not be conceived as physical immortality. Like Buddhism and Hinduism, Taoism believes in the cycle of death and reincarnation. An Immortal (Xian) refers to an enlightened one whose spirit is no longer bound by the cycle of death and reincarnation. The exact history of Immortalism and Taoist Alchemy development is unknown; however, it is known that the meditation practice is based on the principles of psychosomatic harmonization and the psychocosmic relationship from the classic medical doctrine, the *Internal Book (Nei Jing)*.

ALCHEMY

The Heavenly Primal Elixir Meditation is also known as an Internal Elixir Meditation (Nei Dan Fa). Your Lower Dan Tien (a psychic centre 7.5 cm/3 in below your navel area) is symbolically treated as the Alchemy cauldron.

During the meditation, the physical, psychical and spiritual ingredients are gathered, treated and transformed into medicine in the cauldron. These ingredients are Essence of Life (Jing), Primal Universal Energy (Yuen Qi) and Spirit (Shen). These three ingredients are considered as the Three Primal Treasures (San Yuen Bao) of our body. For that reason, Heavenly Primal Elixir Meditation

(Tien Yuen Dan Fa) is also frequently known as the Three Primal Elixir Meditation (San Yuen Dan Fa), referring to the three primal energies of Jing, Qi and Shen within our body.

The circulation of energy, Qi, along the central meridians is the method of gathering the ingredients. They are the Conception Meridian at the front and the Governing Meridian at the back and top half of the head. The gathering of ingredients is symbolized as gathering the medicines (Cai Yao) because the formation of elixir is for healing the body, the mind and the spirit. Your physical, psychical and spiritual selves are nourished and transformed into higher energies and higher inspirations.

Once the medicine is mature, your body and your Spirit will be restored to their pre-natal status. The sequential transformations will rejuvenate your body and subsequently free your Spirit (true self or higher ego) from the bondage with your body to unite with the source of creation, Tao. An enlightened Spirit becomes an Immortal (Xian) as it can command its own destiny of life and death and it is no longer bound by the limitation of space and time or the cycle of rebirth and death.

CHINESE MEDICINE

Taoist Alchemy has a very deep-rooted relationship with Chinese classical medical doctrine. Chinese medicine has a very different approach to its western counterpart. To understand the Alchemy Meditation one needs to have some basic understanding about the Chinese medical concept. In Chinese medicine, the body, mind and spirit are considered as an integral whole. Our physical wellbeing and mental stability are governed by the energy, Qi, harmonization within our body. The body and the mind are in a bipolar relationship to each other. The Qi imbalance of our body (disease) can directly affect the imbalance of our mind and vice versa. The imbalance of our mind is often a direct result of our emotional upheavals caused by our reactions toward the dualistic nature of the world in terms of gain and loss, success and failure or right and wrong. Such emotional turmoil induces fluctuations of Qi flow in our body, as suggested by the Yellow Emperor's *Internal Book* (*Nei Jing*):

Anger induces losing Qi upward.
Excessive happiness slows down Qi flow.
Sadness dissipates Qi.
Worry induces losing Qi downward.
Coldness withdraws Qi flow. Heat disperses Qi.
Shock confuses Qi flow. Weariness wastes Qi.
Excessive thought induces stagnation of Qi flow.

From the Chinese medical point of view, when a man is ill physically, he is also ill psychologically or mentally. When he is ill mentally, he is also depleted in the Spirit. As our modern society is profit-driven, we are conditioned to gain our happiness by personal acquisition of power, material possessions, glory and pride. From a tender age we are encouraged to be a competitive performer and an individual winner. We have been brainwashed by the daily bombardment of commercial media and advertisements encouraging us to conform to certain contemporary trends, follow certain modern fashions and acquire certain brand names. Happiness in our modern society is measured by living fast, indulging superfluously and exhibiting wealth, pride, material possessions, social status and power.

Consequently, we have enslaved ourselves by our egotistic selfishness, boundless desires, unrealistic expectations and excessive material, emotional and physical cravings. When dealing with adversity, our actions become impulsive and our emotions become unstable. Our unfulfilled desires invoke negative emotions such as anger, rage, jealousy, sadness, despair, anxiety and frustration, causing depletion of energy and disharmony. If we waste too much vital emotional and physical energy through negative emotions, excessive physical assertion and superfluous indulgence, a psychosomatic imbalance will be created. Such an imbalance will create illnesses and accelerate ageing.

The Alchemy Meditation brings about a healing process of balancing the physical and emotional energies. This psychosomatic harmonization process is commonly known as 'the restoration of Human Nature (Xing) and Life

(Ming)'. The Human Nature (Xing) is expressed through our heart. Our heart is the centre of boundless desires and expectations. Our expectations and desires stem from our genetics, social conditioning, indoctrination, experience and beliefs. Life (Ming) refers to our vitality, which is expressed through our motivation, virility and physical wellbeing. Fundamentally, restoration of Human Nature (Xing) is to lower our desires and expectations while restoration of Life (Ming) is to repair and to rejuvenate our bodies. The Heavenly Primal Elixir Meditation (Tien Yuen Dan Fa) involves four key stages:

- **Stage one** is to transform Jing (Essence of Life) into Qi (Universal Energy).

- **Stage two** is to transform Qi (Universal Energy) into Shen (Spirit or True Self).

- **Stage three** is to separate the Spirit from the physical body and return to the Void.

- **Stage four** is the unification of the Void with the source of all creation, Tao.

Stage one is called the Microcosmic Cycle (Xiao Zhou Tien) and Stage two is called the Macrocosmic Cycle (Da Zhou Tien). These two stages are the preliminary stages of formation of the Elixir for nourishing the physical body and the Spirit, namely the 'restoration of Xhing and Ming', which we have already discussed above. The last two stages are the maturation of the Elixir leading to the liberation of the Spirit (Shen) and the accomplishment of Immortality through the unification with Tao.

Preparatory Exercises

It is necessary to perform three key massages before attempting phase one of the Heavenly Primal Elixir Meditation, the Microcosmic Cycle (Xiao Zhou Tien).

DRY FACE WASH (CA MIAN)

• Sit with composure, with your body erect.

• Rub your palms together, until they are hot.

• Put your palms over your face and massage your face with a circular movement 36 times. You can do more repetitions if you wish to.

• Pay attention to the tense areas and apply more pressure to soften the tension. Maintain the body's awareness throughout the meditation that follows.

BACK MASSAGE (MO BEI)

• Clench your fists and place them on your back over your kidney areas. Use the back of your fists to massage your kidney areas with a circular movement 36 times.

• This exercise will energize the kidneys to stimulate the emission of Jing energy.

DAN TIEN MASSAGE (MO DAN TIEN)

- Place your right palm over your Lower Dan Tien area, which is 7.5 cm (3 in) below your navel. Massage the Dan Tien centre with an anticlockwise circular movement 36 times.

- Change to the left palm and once again massage the same area clockwise with a circular movement 36 times.

- The Lower Dan Tien acts as a cauldron for storing the transformed energies and turning them into medicine. The aim of this exercise is to prepare and energize the cauldron. The circular massage movements help to activate the internal motions of the energy centre and to induce subsequent automatic Qi circulation.

- You can also greatly heighten your body's awareness if you increase the repetitions of the massage by making the Lower Dan Tien centre very hot and more palpable.

- If you wish to strengthen the internal activity, you can do more complementary exercises at this preparatory phase of your meditation. More complementary exercises can be found in the previous chapter.

- Now put your palms down on your lap and place them into a Tai Chi gesture (Mudra, see page 38) and close your eyes to proceed to the next stage of the meditation.

Stage One:
The Microcosmic Cycle

Primal Jing (Yuen Jing) is a pre-natal finite energy, which we inherit from birth. The first stage of this meditation is to transform Primal Jing into Primal Qi (Yuen Qi), the master building element of the universe. Your body will be rejuvenated when the energy is transformed.

Go through the Deep Relaxation meditation and transfer your attention from the Upper Dan Tien toward the Lower Dan Tien, once you have tuned in internally. There are altogether three Dan Tien centres at the front of your body. These are:

• **The Centre of Eyebrows Point (Yin Tang)** which is located in the mid-point between the eyebrows and is known as the third eye in many eastern religious sects but is known as the upper Dan Tien in Taoist terminology.

• **The Solar Plexus Point (Chung Wan)** is located about 10 cm (4 in) above the navel and is known as the Middle Dan Tien or Middle Field of Elixir.

• **The Lower Dan Tien Point (Kuan Yuen)** is located at the centre of your body, 7.5 cm (3 in) below the navel.

Dan Tien means Field of Elixir. They are centres for storing and transforming energies and Elixir. You don't have to do anything physically but consciously put all of your concentration onto your Lower Dan Tien centre. If you abide by the principle of Wu Wei, Qi will be activated automatically. You may feel sensations of heat, pulsation, vibration, a movement of pearls rolling or electric shocks. When you feel some sensations within, it is an indication of positive progress.

The next hurdle is the opening of the three Gateway (San Guan) points on your vertebrae. They are the Coccyx point, the Middle Back point and the Occipital point. Qi moves down toward the Perineum point and enters the Coccyx point. This is the opening of the first Gateway. Qi may stop at this point for a few days. Gradually, the Middle Gateway and the Upper Gateway points will also be opened, allowing Qi to channel through the meridian. When Qi reaches the Crown point it will set itself in full motion round the central meridians. Don't be anxious if you do not feel anything at the beginning. It might take a few days or longer to set it in motion. Once you can feel some kind of sensations, however small or prominent, do not be distracted by excitement. Allow the energy to circulate in its own time and at its own pace. This first stage of the circulation of energy is called the Microcosmic Cycle (Xiao Zhou Tien). The cultivation of Elixir (Dan) at this stage is called Little Medicine (Xiao Yao).

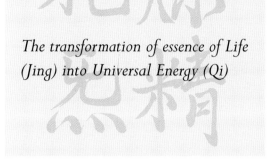

The transformation of essence of Life (Jing) into Universal Energy (Qi)

The following list is the sequential order of the most important energy energizing centres along the Microcosmic Circulation Pathway.

- **The Lower Dan Tien Point (Kuan Yuen)** is located at the centre of your body, 7.5 cm (3 in) below your navel. Lower Dan Tien is also called the Sea of Energy (Qi Hai). This is the storage centre for Jing to transform into Primal Qi. Concentrate on this point at all times and sense the expansion and movement of energy.

- **The Perineum Point** is located in between the genitalia and the anus. The common Chinese names are Yin Meeting (Hui Yin) and Bottom of the Sea (Hai Di) because it is just beneath the Sea of Energy centre (Qi Hai). Lower Dan Tien and Hai Dee have a very close relationship as sometimes you may feel the Qi movements inseparable at these two locations.

- **The Coccyx Point (Chang Chiang)** is located at the tip of the 'tail bones'. This is the first Gateway point on the Governing Meridian.

- **The Kidney Energy Centre** is called the Door of Life (Ming Mun) which is located between the second and the third lumbar vertebrae and it is parallel horizontally to the mid-curve of your waist. As this is the storage

and outlet area of the Jing energy, it is sometimes called the Door of Jing (Jing Mun).

- **The Middle Back Point (Chi Chung)** is located at the eleventh thoracic vertebra. This point is also known as the second Gateway point on the Governing Meridian. Sense the linkage with the first Gateway point at the coccyx by stretching the lower back between them.

- **The Large Vertebra Point (Tai Chui)** is located between the seventh cervical and first thoracic vertebrae. Tai Chui means the large vertebra because the cervical seventh is prominently protruded. Tai Chui is the connective point between the body and the neck.

- **The Occipital Point (Yu Chien)** is the Third Gateway Point on the Governing Meridian and it is also the connection point between the head and the neck. Concentrate on this point by linking up with the other two Gateway Points at the middle back and coccyx by stretching your spine longer and longer. Yu Chien means Jade Pillow.

- **The Crown Point (Pai Hui)** is located centrally on top of the head. Pai Hui means Hundred Gathering. This is the important energy-gathering centre of your body and the psychic doorway to liberating your Spirit (Shen) during the third stage of meditation.

- **The Centre of Eyebrows Point (Yin Tang)** is located in the mid-point between the eyebrows. This point is known as the third eye in many eastern religious sects. This is the Upper

Dan Tien in the Taoist terminology. This point is also called the Doorway of Spirit (Shen Mun) because this is the outlet for expression of your emotions and your consciousness. Concentrate to see beyond sight, to hear beyond sounds and to allow your perception to expand beyond your normal boundaries.

• **The Heart Point (Tan Chung)** is located at the mid-point of the sternum and is level with the fourth intercostal space of the ribcage. It is also level with the nipples in men. This is the psychic centre of your heart where the heart energy is released and gathered during the circulation of Qi. Concentrate on this point to sense openness, honesty, humanity, love and compassion.

• **The Solar Plexus Point (Chung Wan)** is located about 10 cm (4 in) above the navel. This is the Middle Field of Elixir at the stomach region, also known as the Middle Dan Tien. This point is sometimes called the Yellow Room because, according to the Taoist Five Element doctrine, the stomach belongs to the earth element and its colour is yellow. Concentrate on this point to sense determination and courage.

• **The Navel Point (Chi Chung)** is located at the centre of the navel. This is the final passage point before Qi goes back to the Lower Dan Tien point. The cycle is thus completed and starts all over again.

When Qi circulation begins, Jing will be collected from the Ming Mun and the heart energy will also be collected from the heart centre (Tan Chung). Qi circulation will progress to become smoother and more rhythmic after initial occasional stoppages and sluggish motions. Palpable sensations can then be felt in all the energy centres especially the Lower Dan Tien and the perineum areas where a heightened sensual sensation develops. Women may feel a swollen sensation around the labia major and the

The Microcosmic Cycle

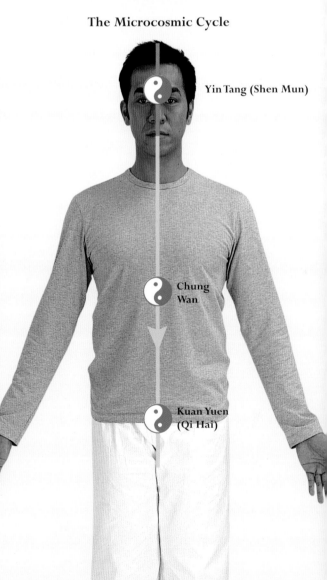

Yin Tang (Shen Mun)

Chung Wan

Kuan Yuen (Qi Hai)

clitoris areas while men may have a penile erection lasting for the whole meditation period or longer.

This phenomenon is called the Rise of Yang Energy (Sheng Yang), which reflects that more sexual energy is transformed as a result of the rejuvenation in progress. You should be neither alarmed nor excited about the Sheng Yang phenomenon. Do not deviate your thought with any sexual fantasy but, instead, carry on with your meditation without breaking your concentration.

Your sexual energy will subsequently be transformed into a higher form of creative energy Yuen Qi. When the higher energy is transformed, the Sheng Yang phenomenon will gradually subside.

This first stage of the Microcosmic Circulation (Xiao Zhou Tien) may last for months or over a year when subsequently a small Elixir (Dan) will be formed as a small pearl of white glow inside your Lower Dan Tien. Hence, the Elixir at this stage is called Little Medicine (Xiao Yao).

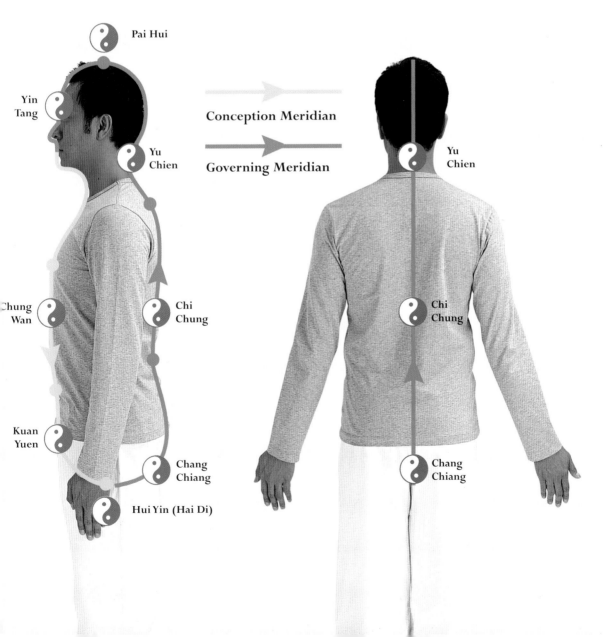

Stage Two: Macrocosmic Cycle

When the Little Medicine (Xiao Yao) is formed, you are now ready to enter the second stage of the Alchemy Meditation. Essentially, the Macrocosmic Circulation and the Microcosmic Circulation are very similar.

You don't need to be consciously aware of how the transformation is done. All you need to do is to follow the same procedures as the first stage of the meditation and allow the Qi to circulate in its own time and at its own pace. As you are progressing, the energy circulation will also get faster and faster along the meridians' pathway and the Elixir will also grow bigger and bigger and become Big Medicine (Da Yao). This fast Qi rotation is traditionally called River Rotation (Hé Chē).

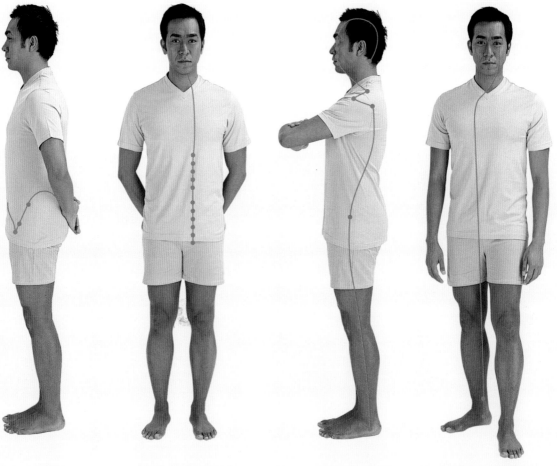

Belt Meridian   **Chung Meridian**   **Yang Chow Meridian**   **Yin Chow Meridian**

Transformation of Universal Energy (Qi) into Spirit or True Self (Shen)

When your mind unwinds and goes further away from external reality, the Internal Scenery (Nei Jing) will become clearer and clearer. Extra meridians will gradually reveal themselves within your body. You don't need to know their exact locations to experience their existence, just keep to the non-action principle, Wu Wei, and the whole network of extra meridians will show themselves eventually. When Big Medicine (Da Yao) forms, there are usually six signs:

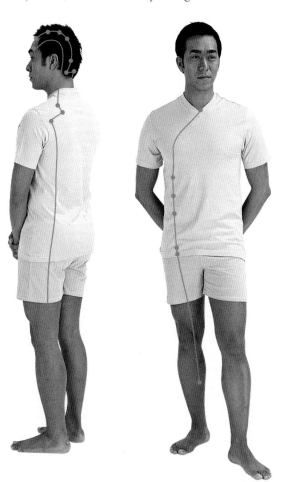

Yang Wai Meridian   **Yin Wai Meridian**

• Burning heat at the Lower Dan Tien

• Burning heat at the kidney region and the Door of Life Point (Ming Mun)

• Bright golden light in front of one's eyes and in the Upper Dan Tien (Yin Tang)

• Sensation of breeze behind one's ears

• Thundering noises in the Occipital Centre (Yu Chien)

• Sensations of water gushing upward from the body with involuntary muscular contraction at the nasal area

You may experience one or all of the phenomena described above or none at all. It is not important whether you have experienced one or all of them or something totally different because these phenomena only reflect the heightening and sharpening of your perceptions. Although they are signs of good progress, they are not the means to an end. You must not dwell on them, or you will be side-stepping onto the path of self complacency and egotism.

The extra meridians of Internal Scenery (Nei Jing) together with the central Conception Meridian and the Governing Meridian form the Macrocosmic Cycle (Dai Zhou Tien). When the Internal Scenery (Nei Jing) reveals itself, just observe it in a peripheral manner and don't allow it to distract your concentration on the Central Meridians and the Lower Dan Tien. If any of the six signs occur, don't be excited and allow them to divert your concentration, as your focus should be solely on the transforming of Qi to Shen on the Central Meridians' pathway.

Who Am I?

To understand the next stage of the meditation, it is necessary to understand the Taoist idea of Soul (Hun) and Spirit (Shen). Spirit (Shen) is your true self, the indestructible ego.

Who is this true self? Who is this ego? Who am I? When people think of themselves, they normally refer to their body, but as long as you can say 'my body', you are merely referring to your body as an external entity, which belongs to you. Your body is only an external representation of yourself, as are your name, your title, your status, your qualifications and so forth. Your body goes through countless mutations and transformations from conception to birth, from cradle to grave, from last incarnation to this incarnation and from this incarnation to the next incarnation. Therefore, your body is not a conclusive you or a constant you.

Some people may think their personality is their true selves. We are all carrying numerous identities and disguises throughout our lives. We have been a son or a daughter, a mother or a father, an uncle or an aunt, a niece or nephew, a teacher or a student, a donor or a recipient, a driver or a passenger, a husband or a wife, a boss or a worker and so on and so forth. While we are wearing the costume as a father, we behave as a father and we speak like a father. While we are facing our father, we behave as a child. While we are wearing the costume as a teacher, we behave as a teacher and we express as a teacher. While we are facing our teacher, we behave as a student. We change our personality, our modes of behaviour, tones of speech,

thinking patterns and social boundaries drastically when we are acting out different parts and playing different roles. We sometimes act the part according to social expectation, sometimes act the part due to circumstantial necessity and sometimes act the part for the sake of acting and pretending. We might change our roles from 20–100 times a day without being conscious of doing so. Therefore, your personality is not your true self either.

Whether you are consciously, subconsciously or unconsciously playing the roles or acting the part, someone is actively engaging in the background observing, thinking and decision-making constantly in your awakened consciousness, your sub-consciousness, your unconsciousness and in your dreams. That person is your true self. A piece of Taoist classic text describes the true self as the master (Zhu Ren) within. However, one can only reclaim ownership as a master if one's Spirit (Shen) is being awakened. When the Big Medicine (Da Yao) is mature, your Spirit (Shen) will be nourished, restored and awakened. A Taoist classic text described this moment symbolically as the formation of the foetus, the pivotal movement of spiritual rebirth when the true self or the enlightened Spirit (Shen) levitates itself from the lesser self (Hun).

The Mystery of Life and Death

Our unenlightened Spirit or Soul (Hun) together with our Physical Vitality (Po) represent the manifestations of our ego in the material world.

Our Soul (Hun) is the Yang element of our ego, which is bound by the physical body when we are on the material plane. Our Soul (Hun) governs our mental activities, creative thoughts, decision-making, intuition and our logical reasoning. Physical Vitality (Po) on the other hand is the Yin element of our ego. It manifests our motivations, our drive, our physical wellbeing and our five senses. Hun and Po consequently govern our physical and mental wellbeing while we are on the material plane. Hun dwells in blood and expresses through our eyes. Po derives from Essence of Life (Jing) and expresses through the wellbeing of our physique, our physical energy, our motivations and our drive. Therefore, if you suffer from anaemia, you might also carry other symptoms such as weariness, inability to concentrate, forgetfulness and inability to make decisions quickly. And, if you were sick, your Po would also be affected, resulting in low vitality, lack of strength and loss of motivation.

At one's natural death, both Hun and Po leave the physical carcass. Po sinks to the earth and dissolves into oblivion while Hun enters into an after-life subterranean dimension commonly known as Hell (Di Fu) or Supreme Yin (Tai Yin). The Taoist Hell cannot be equated to the Christian's eternal torturing domain. It is a transitional period between death and rebirth. If one dies from an accidental death, Hun and Po will not separate and the Soul will become an earth-bound apparition haunting at the location of its death. It will not enter the subterranean dimension until it has been redeemed to rest in peace by offering burial or cremation and prayers. On entering the subterranean dimension, Hun then becomes a Deceased Soul (You Hun) or Ghost (Gui). Its memory and its expectation of how to represent itself shape its body in this dimension. Most Ghosts prefer to represent themselves with a more youthful body instead of the old and diseased one before their passing.

The environment in this dimension will also be shaped according to the Ghosts' desires, their memory of their last incarnation and their attachment to the material life. Most Ghosts mirror the physical environment of what they were accustomed to while they were on the earth plane. Some Ghosts may even create a better environment, which

they were deprived from or longed for when they were on the earth plane. They may go through a period of torturous purgatory, of retribution, to redeem and correct their wrongdoings. They may also enjoy a period of rest and good life if they were righteous and charitable in their last incarnations. Some may even dwell on a higher stratum of the subterranean world, depending on the merits of their good doings.

Some Taoist Religious Sects (Tao Jiao) believe that there are nine Realms of Hell and each Realm is subdivided into four Domains giving a total of 36 Domains. In fact, these periods of events, geographical locations, material and physical realities in the subterranean dimension are all internal realities created by one's own consciousness, according to one's own belief, memory, emotional and material attachments. A torturous purgatory is the reflection of retribution from one's repentant conscience. Your emotional and material attachments will subsequently gravitate you toward another incarnation by entering into a new womb (Tou Tai). However, if on the other hand you strive for a higher self and practise meditation during your lifetime, you can levitate the status of Soul (Hun) by awakening the dormant Spirit (Shen) and become an Immortal (Xian).

Stage Three: Transformation of Spirit to Return to the Void

On entering this stage of meditation, the medicine will become mature and grow bigger. The mature Big Medicine (Da Yao) will gradually rise from the Lower Dan Tien area toward the Upper Dan Tien area (mid-point between your eyebrows) to nourish your Spirit (Shen).

It may rise to the Middle Dan Tien first or it may rise directly to the Upper Dan Tien. The Upper Dan Tien is also called the Doorway of Spirit (Shen Mun) because this is the outlet centre for the manifestation of Spirit (Shen), in other words for emotions and any activities of consciousness.

THE SIX GREAT SPIRIT COMMUNICATIONS

Your psychic senses may also suddenly be awakened as a result of entering this altered state of perception. These psychic abilities are called the Six Great Spirit Communications (Liu Da Shen Tong). The Chinese word 'Tong' literally means communication or channelling, which refers to the psychical communication abilities of the enlightened Spirit (Shen). When the Spirit (Shen) separates from the physical body and returns to the Void (Xu), its psychic faculties are awakened and its abilities to perceive, to act and to communicate become boundless and cannot be obstructed by time, space, distance, geographical locations, matters or anti-matters. These psychic powers will further increase when the enlightened Spirit has gone through the final stage of the great union with the Void (Xu)

when the Immortal and the Creative Source Tao become one. The Six Great Spirit Communications (psychic abilities) are as follows:

• **Celestial Eyes Communication (Tien Yan Tong)** This power includes the abilities of clairvoyance, remote viewing and seeing the cause and effect of an event in its past, present and future.

• **Life Understanding Communication (Su Ming Tong)** This power includes the ability of understanding the causality of events and the ability to remember past incarnations.

• **Other Hearts Communication (Tar Xin Tong)** This power includes the abilities of mind reading, telepathy and heightened intuition.

• **Super Legs Communication (Shen Zu Tong)** This power is the ability of astro-travelling; travelling through time and space in all dimensions. This ability also enables the Immortals to enter into people's dreams to deliver messages.

*Transformation Spirit or True Self
(Shen) to return to Void (Xu)*

- **Celestial Ears Communication (Tien
Er Tong)** This power includes the abilities of
clairaudience and remote hearing.

- **Leak and Dissipation Communication
(Leu Jeen Toon)** This power is the ability to
withhold the dissipation of energy so as to slow
down the ageing process of the physical body
and allow the Immortals to function on the
earth plane for a long time.

SPIRITUAL AWAKENING

The awakening of these powers is just a side effect
of the spiritual awakening and advancement of the
Yang Spirit (Shen). You must not consciously
attempt to pursue this psychic power gain or you
will be falling into a dangerous and erroneous
path of egotism. Your desire to explore your
newly found abilities could hinder you from your
spiritual advancement. If you investigate the
opening of these psychic faculties as your only
reason for practising the Taoist meditation, you
are on the wrong path. Remember, Taoists never
consciously search for power and egotistical
control. If people are consciously searching for
psychic supremacy, they will invoke the egotistical
lower self, the Yin Spirit (Yin Shen), or the
unenlightened Soul (Hun). The psychic powers
from the Yin Spirit are those of a mediumistic
nature, which deal with ghosts and demons. It is

also a very dangerous pursuit as the dividing line
between the psychic and psychiatric is very
narrow. People who search for a low level of
psychic power could venture into dangerous
waters and become mentally ill.

If you put all your concentration into
nourishing your spirit, your Soul (Hun) will
migrate toward higher aspirations. Your Spirit
(Shen) will become awakened and transformed, as
your ego inclines toward selflessness. You will
gradually let go of your old mode of self, habitual
pride, emotional attachment, prejudices and self-
importance and free your Spirit from the bondage
and the gravitational pull of lower desires, egotism,
material attachment, emotional attachment and the
physical attachment of your body.

A new sense of understanding will gradually
blossom within your consciousness and the
awakened Spirit (Shen) will set itself free in a gush
of golden light toward the Crown centre (Pai Hui).
When this happens, do not be excited or scared but
follow the principle of non-action (Wu Wei) and be
a silent observer. Your Spirit (Shen) may look down
at your body from above, amid the radiance of
golden light, and a flood of knowledge and wisdom
will suddenly ignite and reveal itself to you. Initially,
you may even feel a sense of remoteness in viewing
and controlling your body. As you progress, your
Spirit (Shen) will suddenly experience the all-
embracing great Void where all creations begin and
end. In the midst of profound motionless quietude,
emptiness and timelessness, there is a new sense of
freshness, recognition, maturity and connectivity at
the awakening spiritual rebirth. Like the reunion
when a child, believing herself to be an orphan,
embraces her mother for the first time, this is the
most profound, most blessed moment.

Stage Four: Unification of the Void and Tao

This is when your Spirit (Shen) is free and has returned to the Void. The final transformation will happen in a twinkle of a moment when one becomes all and all becomes one.

No earthly word or phrase can be adequate to describe this divine experience of celestial unification when the Mother (Tao) and Child (Void) become one. In this moment of transcendental oneness, time, space, physical and metaphysical dimensions integrate and disintegrate into all beings and nothingness. Perceiving is being perceived. Creation is being created. The beginning is the same as the ending. Goodness is the same as evil. Light is the same as darkness. Now is the same as eternity. There is only one divine sense of understanding – an understanding when the Immortal and the eternal Tao are one.

Unification of the Void (Xu) and Tao

Nothingness ([Wu], referring to the condition of the Void) is the origin of the universe, while, Reality (Yau) is the mother of myriad beings. Therefore, when one contemplates within the Nothingness, the enigma can be observed, and when one contemplates within its Reality the bounds can be observed. Both are from the same source with different names, the same source of all mystery, the gateway of all wonderment.

TAO TE JING

Common Questions

Q **Should I practise the Alchemy Meditation on my own or could I practise with other people?**

Unless the people you are practising with have the same motivation and commitment as you have, it could be inconvenient and hinder your progress. Meditation is a spiritual quest and not a social event. Therefore, it is more advantageous to find your own solitude and establish your own sanctuary.

Q **I read from other sources about the Microcosmic Cycle (Xiao Zhou Tien) and Qi Gong, which mapped out more Qi centres than the ones described in this book. Why?**

The Qi centres described in this book are universally used according to the classical sources. Different schools or different teachers might have different preferences for the Qi centres. However, most of them would use similar ones, especially the three Gateway centres and the three Field of Elixir centres as well as the Crown centre and the Perineum Point.

Q **I read from other sources about the Microcosmic Orbit (Cycle), which describes the Navel centre as the Lower Dan Tien. Why?**

According to Taoist archive and classical medical literature, Lower Dan Tien (Kuan Yuen) is the area 7.5 cm (3 in) below the Navel centre (Chi Chung). Lower Dan Tien is also called Sea of Energy (Qi Hai) because this is the storage area of Primal Energy, which has a close relationship with our sexual function. The author who describes Navel centre as Lower Dan Tien appears to have adopted the western concept of pre-natal origin, which is based on the idea of the umbilicus as a pre-natal linkage with the mother's womb. The Chinese physiological concept is not the same as its western counterpart, therefore we adhere to classical medical doctrine.

Q **Since practising the Microcosmic Cycle, my libido has increased. Is this normal?**

Microcosmic Cycle is a rejuvenation process, therefore; as your body regains its juvenility, your virility will also be restored to a more youthful state. This indicates good progress. Listen to the natural demands from your body and don't over-or under-tax your body functions. This applies to all other bodily functions including sex and reproduction. Remember, an over used machine gets worn and malfunctions while an under-used machine gets rusty and will subsequently cease to work.

Q **What should I see or feel when the Internal Scenery (Nei Jung) reveals itself?**

Nai Jien refers to the other six extra Qi Meridians. Similar sensations to those felt on the Microcosmic pathway on the Central Meridians such as heat, pulsation, vibration, a pearl rolling sensation or electric shocks may be felt. It is quite common to neither feel nor see the Internal Scenery at all. It is not important because the Internal Scenery is only the side effect of an altered state of perception, which is momentary and illusory. Dwelling on these phenomena will only impede your progress. Remember, abide with non-action (Wu Wei) and nothing will be left undone.

Q **I have been practising Microcosmic Cycle for a few months now but how do I know when it is the right time to progress to the next stage of my meditation practice?**

You don't need to know when, as no time is the right time. If you abide by the principle of Wu Wei, the transitional periods of the four stages are very blurred. At the right moment of transformation, the meditation will progress. All you need to do is to let go, relax and keep your concentration at the Lower Dan Tien area. Nature knows when and Qi will move in its own time, at its own pace. The time span between the four stages will vary from person to person. Some people may practise for months or years before experiencing advancement. Others may take just a few days to achieve results.

THE *Living* TAO

THE TAOIST LIFESTYLE

Ancient Taoists lived a simple hermitic life in a blissful natural environment among the forests, rivers and mountains. They lived in total self-sufficiency by growing their own crops, rearing their own animals, and picking fruit, vegetables, medicinal herbs, edible fungi, nuts and seeds from their natural surroundings.

Their diet may have been largely from vegetable and fungus sources with supplements from their farmed egg and dairy produce as well as fish from the river. Based on the writings of Chuang Tzu and his contemporaries, a vegetarian diet appeared to be practised for special rites only. Subsequently, Taoist vegetarianism may have been borrowed from Buddhism. There is also evidence that some Taoists avoided eating rhizome or root tuber such as potatoes and yams. This was due to a general misconception that eating potatoes and yams could deplete Qi through belching and passing wind.

Fasting was also widely practised as part of the Alchemy routines to cleanse internal energy (Qi) and to access higher consciousness. When they were not fasting, Taoists also disciplined themselves to eat a light diet. Their daily farming routines kept their bodies constantly active. Their excursions to collect medicinal herbs often required climbing steep mountains and walking a long way into the woods and forests. The climbing and long-distance walks provided very high-quality exercises for strengthening their muscles and ligaments as well as compacting their bones. The high-altitude atmosphere provided quality clean air for healthy lungs. Their organic farming and food from the natural surroundings also provided them with a healthy and nutritious diet. This carefree, non-competitive

and natural way of living thus contributed to their good health and longevity.

The ancient Taoist way is no longer viable in our modern culture. Modern living complicates our lives with political, social and environmental factors. Today, you are required to follow the structure of society and abide by its laws and regulations. You are no longer able to erect your dwelling in the place of your choice unless you are the owner of the land and, even then, you will have to face planning laws. You are no longer able to farm or to fish without legal ramifications. Our air is no longer clean and pure. Our atmosphere is depleted. Our rivers are polluted with industrial wastes, sewage and chemicals. The natural order of our foodstuffs, the structure and growth pattern, has been altered chemically, mechanically and genetically. Our food supply is largely inorganic, processed and contains health-hazardous additives, insecticides, herbicides and fertilizers. Our living environments are noisy, stressful, competitive, over-crowded and compartmental. Even if circumstances permit you to live like an ancient Taoist, you no longer will be able to duplicate the quality of their natural environment.

The way of Tao is ever-transforming and a modern Taoist must adapt to change. Be vigilant about personal issues such as health, hygiene, nutrition, drugs and medication. Be proactive toward global issues such as modern farming methods, environmental depletion, animal welfare, world trade and ecology. Looking after mother earth is looking after yourself. Whatever you have taken from mother earth you must in some way repay so as to make your gain sustainable. As your personal health is affected by social, environmental and political influences, you need to understand and tackle the wider issues of global imbalance and universal malady. As consumers, we should demand green products. As scientists, consider adopting the Wu Wei principle to work with nature instead of conquering it. As businessmen, think about working toward fair trade in the developing world. As politicians, contemplate tackling global issues of health, education, environment and poverty. Mutual responsibility and fair sharing among all will enable common gains in health, wealth, peace and stability worldwide. The world is changing and integrating so rapidly that a modern Taoist can no longer be an isolated hermit without contributing and engaging with the world at large.

Food and Drink

The World Health Organization has described obesity as a 'global epidemic'
with an estimated 250 million obese people worldwide.

In the USA, over one third of the adult population
is obese, rising to more than 50 per cent in some
ethnic minorities. Since 1980 the proportion of
obese people in the United Kingdom has risen
almost three times. Obesity can cause heart
disease, diabetes, breast cancer and colon cancer.

If you want to prolong your life, you must
understand that we do not live to eat but we eat
to live. This does not mean that you are not
allowed to enjoy food. It means that you must not
allow the craving for food to take over your life.
Listen to your body, eat only when you are
hungry and not when you are craving for
something tasty. Modern food manufacturers add
brighter colours, refined sugar, salt and flavour
enhancers to excite your visual reflex, odour
reflex and your taste buds so that you want to go
back for more. They use harmful chemicals such
as preservatives and antioxidants to prolong shelf
life. Their advertisements bombard your brain
with subliminal information to make you believe
that you are lagging behind the modern culture
unless you drink certain soft drinks or eat certain
types of fast food. Consuming such chemicals and
additives can exhaust your liver causing allergies,
headaches, depression, aggression, hyperactivity
and behavioural problems as well as premature
tooth decay, cardiovascular disease and cancers.

If you want to live a long and healthy life, you
must endeavour to eat fresh, natural, organic food
and eliminate fast foods, fatty foods, refined
foods, comfort foods, artificial foods and food
containing unnatural additives from your diet. As
a consumer, your predilection and your demand
for natural and organic produce can affect the
change of culture and vision from the food
producers and food manufacturers. You must not
assume that all edible food in the supermarket is
harmless to your health.

ADDITIVES
• Most artificial colourings are derivatives from
coal tar, for example tartrazine (E102), sunset
yellow (E110) and brown FK (154) which may
cause allergies, asthma, hyperactivity, behaviour
change and cancers.

• Nitrites and nitrates such as potassium nitrite
(E249) and potassium nitrate (E252) are used to
inhibit botulism and enhance flavour and colour
of cured meat products such as ham and
sausages. Nitrites and nitrates can cause nausea,
vomiting, dizziness, headaches and hypotension.
When nitrites mix with natural body chemicals
amines, they become highly carcinogenic
chemicals known as nitrosamines.

• Trans fats are generally known as margarine or
hydrogenated fats. Trans fats raise the body's
low-density lipoprotein level, a bad cholesterol,

and simultaneously lower high-density lipoprotein, a good cholesterol, upsetting your natural cholesterol balance. Trans fats are active ingredients in pizza dough, pastry, biscuits and cakes.

- Refined sugar is a metabolic poison, which triggers symptoms of addictive dependency. It is absorbed into your circulation very quickly, inciting insulin secretion from the pancreas to lower the glucose in your blood. The erratic insulin levels lead to conditions of sugar craving, exhaustion, depression, irritability, anxiety and headaches. Consuming excessive refined sugar makes you vulnerable to diabetes and obesity in the long term.

- Calorie-free sugar substitute is not a healthy choice in your diet. Artificial sweeteners such as aspartame (E951), acesulfame K (E950) and saccharin (E954) may increase cancer risk in humans.

- Sulphur dioxide (E220) and sodium sulphite (E221) are used as preservatives and antioxidants in both food and drink. It is now widely accepted that sulphites can induce allergic and asthmatic reactions.

- Monosodium glutamate, a flavour enhancer, can cause allergic reactions including palpitations, muscle tightening, headaches, dizziness, chest pains, depression, mood swings and migraine symptoms. MSG is normally found in packets of crispy snacks, sauces, pork pies, packet soup and pot noodles. It is also widely used by Chinese restaurants, which gave rise to a condition known as Chinese Restaurant Syndrome.

- Preservatives such as BHA (E320), BHT (E321) and EDTA (E385) are widely used in sachet marinade, dry savoury rice, vegetable oil, crisps, dehydrated mashed potato, breakfast cereal, chewing gum and granulated gravy. They can commonly cause allergic reactions and hyperactivity.

- Artificial flavours used in both food and drinks are generally chemical agents, which replicate the odours and tastes of natural food. Like artificial colourings, they can cause allergies, asthma, hyperactivity and behaviour change.

- Excessive salt is widely used by the food manufacturers to excite our taste buds. Our bodies require about 2,500 mg of sodium per day. One teaspoon of salt has about 2,400 mg of sodium. However, it does not necessarily suggest that we require a teaspoon of salt a day because we can also obtain sodium from other food sources. Excessive intake of salt can cause stress, fluid retention, hypertension and heart disease.

SATURATED FATS

Our body requires cholesterol to build cell walls and construct certain body chemicals. However, excessive cholesterol in our body can be harmful and life-threatening. High levels of cholesterol in blood can cause brittle blood vessels, blocked arteries, coronary heart disease and strokes. Saturated fats are found in meat, butter, margarine, lard, dairy products, biscuits, cakes, pastry and chocolate.

FRIED FOOD

In Spring 2002, Swedish scientists discovered acrylamide, a carcinogenic substance, which made headlines. Several other European countries also corroborated Sweden's discovery. Acrylamide forms from raw ingredients during traditional cooking methods such as frying or baking, the longer the cooking at high temperatures, the more acrylamide will be formed. Acrylamide causes cancer in test animals, which strongly suggests that acrylamide can also cause cancer in humans. Eating fried food is a double jeopardy to your health. It is wise to avoid eating high-fat food anyway and now you have got yet another compelling reason to pass on the fatty potato chips and other 'goodies'.

REFINED FOOD

Modern high-heat milling processes remove the nutritional rich germ and bran from whole wheat grains leaving only a nutritionally poor starch as refined flour. Consequently, refined carbohydrate foods such as pasta, white bread and cereals contain little or no fibre and the natural nutrients that wholegrain foods provide. Refined starch acts like refined sugar, which provides low nutritional

calories while causing glucose imbalance and insulin disturbances. Consuming refined starchy food can increase the health risk of diabetes and heart disease.

The depletion of wheatgerm takes away the essential anti-ageing vitamin E. Lack of dietary fibre in a white starch diet is the major cause of constipation and diverticulitis. Dietary fibre is essential for bulking and softening stools. It is estimated that in North America, a third of people over the age of 45 have diverticulitis. It is also estimated that one in every 14 people in the United Kingdom has constipation at any one time, and that one in ten of those constipated puts up with it.

A VEGETARIAN DIET

Modern intensive factory rearing and battery farming together with force feeding of antibiotics and steroids are not only causing immense suffering to farmed animals but are also detrimental to their physical and mental health. The meat products from these highly drugged, highly stressed, physically damaged and mentally ill animals may in turn cause immeasurable health implications to the human consumers. Overwhelming evidence from research from all over the world has corroborated the health benefits of a vegetarian diet as opposed to an omnivore diet, including:

• Reduction of cardiovascular disease by lowering cholesterol levels

• Reduction of cancer risk including colon cancer, prostate cancer and breast cancer

• Reduction of diet-related diabetes and hypertension

• Reduction of health problems related to obesity

• Minimizing the development of kidney and gall stones

• Minimizing the development of osteoporosis through high dietary acidity and calcium loss in urine

• Avoiding fatal diseases such as Creutzfeldt-Jakob disease (CJD) and food poisoning

A well-balanced vegetarian diet should include grains, peas, beans, mushrooms, nuts, seeds, fruit, seaweeds and vegetables, especially the ones with green leaves, together with eggs, cottage cheese and other dairy products.

Avoid consuming too many dairy products because they are difficult to digest and can cause allergic symptoms such as asthma and eczema. Substitute your protein with quorn (mycoprotein) tofu and soya products. Soya contains flavonoids and polyphenols, which have the ability to slow down bone loss, to counteract hormone-related cancers and to reduce hot flushes during menopause. Soya milk is an excellent alternative to cow's milk, especially for vegans or if you suffer from lactose intolerance.

FASTING AND DETOXIFICATION

Fasting while drinking herbal decoctions to aid the advancement of meditation has long been a prevalent practice in the Taoist tradition. Fasting allows your organs to have a good rest and bring about revitalization to improve Qi harmonization of your body. When you abstain from food, your body has to use the reserved body fats to generate energy and heat. This in turn will also release the trapped toxins from the fatty tissues, which subsequently will be excreted through the urinary system.

Occasionally skipping a meal or performing a partial fast while consuming a light broth or salad are the more practical ways to perform a fast without interfering with your modern daily routine. You can certainly perform a full fast if you plan ahead and perform it during the period of your annual leave or holiday seasons. Don't fast for more than three days, unless you are on a long vacation, because you will require a period of time to get back to your normal routine. When you fast, you will also need to rest physically. Perhaps devote more time to meditation and Qi Gong exercises during the fasting period. Chinese Herbal Tonic and green drinks (vegetable or wheat grass juices) can be drunk liberally during the fasting period to detoxify your body and improve Qi flow. (See the herbs and supplements chapter, pages 120–121 for blood purifier/detoxifier formulas.)

ANTIOXIDANTS – THE INGREDIENTS FOR ETERNAL YOUTH

When a cut apple turns brown or when cooking oil turns rancid, it is due to a chemical reaction called oxidation.

Chemicals called free radicals cause oxidation. The majority of free radicals are released in our body when cells turn food and oxygen into energy. Free radicals may also come from cigarette smoke, pollution and exposure to radiation. They set off a chain reaction in the cells, which can damage proteins, membranes and genetic material. If free radicals form faster than the body can break them down, damage to cells and tissues can occur. Antioxidants help to counteract the free radical damage by firstly preventing the formation of free radicals and secondly reducing the free radical destruction.

• Vitamin C and vitamin E have a rejuvenating effect on all endocrine activities including the sex glands for hormone production. The best sources of vitamin C are from fresh fruits and vegetables when they are eaten raw. Good sources of vitamin E can be found in wheatgerm, seeds, nuts, olives, and green, leafy vegetables.

• Beta-carotene and flavonoids are non-toxic vitamin A, which can be found in carrots, tomatoes, dark green leafy vegetables, red

peppers, sweet potatoes, red berries and soya. Vitamin A is essential for oxygenation of the cells and it improves permeability of the blood capillaries. Flavonoids can reduce wrinkles, protecting the eyes from both cataracts and macular degeneration.

• Antioxidant enzymes are found in sprouted grains, seeds and legumes. They are essential for tackling harmful free radical molecules.

• Selenium, a trace element, can be found in oily fish, such as salmon, and in nuts. The best supplement sources are brewer's yeast and kelp. Selenium is responsible for healthy arteries and circulation and counters the development of cancer.

COOKING UTENSILS AND COOKING METHODS

Aluminium is not a stable metal as it reacts to salt and heat or other food ingredients to form poisonous chemicals. The United States Department of Health and Human Services reports aluminium may be linked to Alzheimer's disease because high levels of aluminium are found in the brains of Alzheimer's patients. Use stainless steel and glass utensils as healthier options.

Prolonged cooking can destroy a food's natural nutrients and minimize its electro-magnetic efficiency. Quick stir-frying and quick steaming are preferable methods. Food such as nuts, mushrooms, fruits and vegetables provide most nutrition when they are eaten raw. Avoid deep-frying food and use only fresh cold-pressed oil.

AVOID DRINKING UNFILTERED TAP WATER

Although water companies follow tight government health and safety guidelines, in the absence of national drinking water quality and safety standards, quality of drinking water varies according to geographical locations. In some places water may still be running through outdated pipework made from lead. Contamination may also occur when water sources are too near to chemical plants or intensive farming areas where pesticides and fertilizers are applied on a vast scale. Chlorine used for water treatment not only causes an unpleasant taste and smell but it might also involve health risks because of the formation of carcinogenic by-products.

Fluoridation of tap water for preventing dental decay in children has also raised doubt and controversy. Research evidence demonstrates that fluoride causes many serious diseases including osteosarcoma. Although water companies assure us that tap water is safe to drink, the long-term health risks cannot be ignored. Therefore, never drink any tap water without filtering the impurities first. Most cartridge filtering systems on the market can filter out 96–99 per cent of the impurities while an osmotic filtering system can filter out almost 100 per cent of the impurities. Always boil filtered water before drinking it, as bacteria and fungus may develop in the absence of chlorine.

THE TAOIST LIFESTYLE **97**

KICK THE HABIT

A western liberal attitude has created an illusion of acceptability for social drug abuse. In fact, social drugs, such as cigarettes, alcohol and marijuana, are the biggest social diseases in our western societies. Very often they are an introduction to harder drug addiction and serious crime. Lung cancer is the most common cancer in men and the second most common cancer in women causing 37,000 deaths a year in the UK. Smoking is responsible for over 31,000 of these deaths. Smoking can also cause oesophagal cancer, laryngeal cancer, and bladder and kidney cancers. People who drink alcohol and smoke have a much higher risk of oesophagal cancer and laryngeal cancer. Free radicals created from smoking can damage your cellular structure, accelerating premature ageing and make your skin wrinkle. Contrary to the advertising, which often features macho images, smoking can destroy your manhood and cause impotence in men.

It is a common misconception that alcohol is a more benevolent social vice. Numerous studies indicate an association between alcohol consumption and aggressive behaviour, especially in people with antisocial personality disorder (ASPD) who are more susceptible to alcohol-related aggression. Continuous drinking will exhaust your liver resulting, in the formation of fibrous scar tissue, cirrhosis and even cancer of the liver.

Marijuana, under the guise of grass, hemp, pot or cannabis, is often described as a herbal relaxant. Many marijuana smokers believe that smoking pot is less harmful than smoking cigarettes or drinking alcohol. This gives them the false security that smoking pot is healthy. A Swedish study revealed that there is a relative risk of developing schizophrenia through smoking marijuana. Smoking marijuana is actually inhaling polycyclic aromatic hydrocarbons and carbon monoxide, which will encourage cancer growth.

All these social vices take away your self-control and undermine your willpower so that you may become dependent on them. This does not go well with the practising of Taoist Alchemy, which encourages you to try to free your body, your mind and your spirit from all external desires and influences. If you want to have a long and productive life, you must kick the habit!

Keep Your Body Moving

It is now known that exercise stimulates the pituitary gland to secrete a natural hormone, beta-endorphin, into the bloodstream. Beta-endorphin is a natural opiate, which produces a 'high' similar to that from morphine. It is believed that the endorphin may also be one of the factors in regulating the release of human growth hormone (HGH).

HGH is a natural hormone which controls the growth of bones and muscles, reproductive and endocrine functions, body and organ functions, enzyme functions and neural functions, as well as cellular and tissue repair. As we age, the release of HGH will also gradually decrease. Most people will have approximately 80 per cent less HGH by the age of 60 compared to when they were 20. Therefore, exercise has positive anti-ageing effects because it increases the levels of HGH.

The natural release of HGH will stimulate fat loss, increase muscle mass and bone density, revitalize sexual and endocrine functions, rejuvenate the complexion, improve circulation, strengthen cardiovascular functions, improve sleep quality and expand memory and cognition. Furthermore, exercising is the best and quickest natural way to dissipate the stress-causing 'unused adrenaline' hormone in your bloodstream that your body may have released from your daily fight or flight response.

AEROBIC EXERCISES

Aerobic exercises involve continuous body movements over a period of time, which gradually increase your heart rate as you are exercising. Therefore, aerobic exercises are essential for burning excessive body fats and strengthening cardiovascular functions. Examples of aerobic exercises are:

• Jogging, including work on the treadmills or elliptical trainers

• Ball games, such as netball, tennis, table tennis, basketball, squash, badminton and soccer

• Swimming and water sports

• Cycling, including work on exercise bikes

• Rowing, including work on rowing machines

Most modern exercise machines contain a combination computer/monitor for measuring your heart rates, distance, calories used, time and speed. Elliptical trainers are the current best indoor aerobic exercise machines because they combine running, stepping, stair-climbing and cycling exercises into one single machine. The elliptical rotation also enables natural body movements of your hip joints and allows your arms and your upper body to work simultaneously. You can also perform backward movements to work on other muscle groups as well as your co-ordination. The ability to adjust variable tension and resistance will enable you to step up the programme as you are progressing.

As you increase the pace of aerobic exercise your heart rate will also increase, with demands for more oxygen as a result. The increase of oxygen from the quick-pumping heart and lungs will combine with your body fats and burn away as energy. This burning fats effect will continue even after you have finished exercising because your metabolic rates will be increased as a result of the aerobic exercises. Use the table below to measure your initial fitness level and monitor your progress as you advance subsequently. You are required to monitor your pulse rates while exercising and your objective is to maintain the 'target heart rate' between 50 and 75 per cent of the maximum heart rate for your age group.

TARGET HEART RATE

Age group	Target heart rate between 50 and 75 % (beats per minute)	Average maximum heart rate of 100 % (beats per minute)
20 years	100–150 bpm	200 bpm
25 years	98–146 bpm	195 bpm
30 years	95–142 bpm	190 bpm
35 years	93–138 bpm	185 bpm
40 years	90–135 bpm	180 bpm
45 years	88–131 bpm	175 bpm
50 years	85–127 bpm	170 bpm
55 years	83–123 bpm	165 bpm
60 years	80–120 bpm	160 bpm
65 years	78–116 bpm	155 bpm
70 years	75–113 bpm	150 bpm
75 years	72–110 bpm	145 bpm
80 years	70–105 bpm	140 bpm
85 years	68–102 bpm	135 bpm
90 years	65–98 bpm	130 bpm

ANAEROBIC EXERCISES

Anaerobic exercises are exercises that involve short periods of strenuous exercise, followed by a short period of rest. Anaerobic activities are normally weight-bearing exercises with muscle-building components. These exercises help to compact bones, sculpt the body shape and to build and strengthen muscles. Examples of anaerobic exercises include:

• Push-ups, pull-ups and stomach crunches

• Weight training

• Glide board low-impact multi-gym exercises

• Isometric exercises

If you prefer to train at home, there are ample home gymnasium products on the market at very reasonable prices. The benefit is that you only pay once with the initial investment against sessional payment and annual membership if you attend a gymnasium. Glide board low-impact multi-gym machines are excellent for anaerobic exercise because they targets all muscle groups of the body to improve strength, endurance and flexibility as well as cardiovascular endurance.Glide boards provide full support to your body while minimizing compression impacts on your joints and back. Because you only allow the gravitational pull to provide resistance for strengthening and stretching your muscles, you can improve flexibility without asserting any unnecessary stress on your body.

If you live in an apartment, an isometric home exercising device could be a better choice for you. Over two hundred experiments conducted over a ten year period discovered that maximum muscle growth can be attained by exerting 60 per cent of existing muscle strength against a superior resistance for only seven seconds daily. It was also found that the isometric training group improved three times faster against the group using conventional training techniques, in terms of strength, endurance, co-ordination and agility.

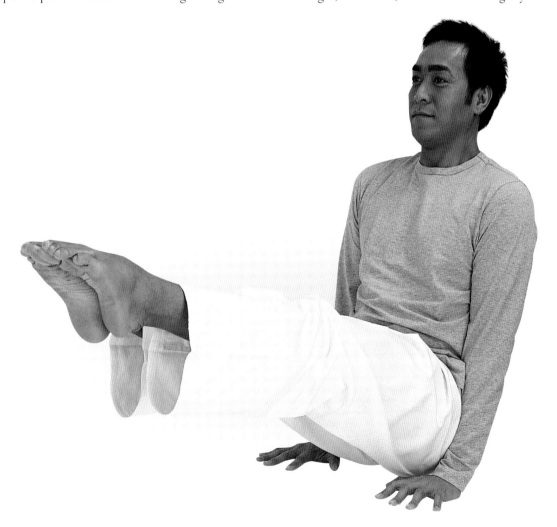

WATCH YOUR BACK

Backache has become a common ailment since man stood up and took his first step in evolution. Between 30 and 40 per cent of the United Kingdom's population have backache symptoms and between 80 and 90 per cent of the population experience backache at some time in their lives. Back problems are costing the nation nearly six billion pounds per year in terms of medical treatment, benefits and production loss. Many of the back problems are caused by stress reflex, bad postures, obesity and injury through lifting with an incorrect posture. Backache is a disabling ailment, which can put sufferers totally out of action. However, with a bit of common sense, a lot of awareness, some hard work and a little help, backache can be totally eliminated.

• Do complementary exercises to stretch and rotate your back. Do weight-bearing exercises to strengthen your back and your abdominal muscles. Alternatively, Tai Chi, yoga and the Alexander Technique are also excellent for correcting the posture and strengthening the supportive muscles as well as maintaining good health.

• Eat sensibly and combine diet and exercise to keep your body to an optimum weight. If you are overweight, you are likely to suffer problems from your back, knees and ankles.

• Pay attention to your posture and maintain a good bearing at all times. A lot of backaches are caused by abnormal curvature (scoliosis), a condition developed from stress reflex and bad sitting or standing postures over a period of time. Find a

practitioner of the Alexander Technique to correct your posture and improve your awareness of it.

- If you have a chronic back problem, visit an osteopath or a chiropractor to realign the subluxation (commonly known as slipped disc) before the condition gets worse. Subluxations can cause other problems to your body because they can interfere with and impede the nerve impulses travelling from your brain via the spinal cord to various parts of your body.

- If you suffer from osteoarthritis of the back, take glucosamine and chondroitin tablets to repair the damage to the cartilage. Also take cod liver oil or flax seed oil as the Omega-3 fatty acids in these oils can reduce cartilage degradation and inflammation in arthritic joints.

- Wearing high-heeled shoes encourages a back arching posture in order to maintain balance and to avoid tipping forward. The arching posture causes unusual stress on your feet and lower back, leading to subsequent displacement of the vertebrae and RSI (repetitive strain injuries) to your feet. Also, when you position your body in

such an unnatural posture, you may bring about premature wear and tear to your hip joints, lower back, feet, knees and ankles through misusing your body repetitively. If you want your joints to function for a long time to come, wear something sensible to walk in.

- We spend on average a third of our lifetime asleep in bed; therefore, it is absolutely crucial to sleep on a bed that is able to support our bodies. If you sleep on an uneven mattress, your spine will be out of alignment causing vertebral displacement in the long term. If your mattress is ten years or older, it is likely that the springs on the mattress are uneven or losing tensile strength, so, it is time to splash out to save your back and get a good night's sleep. A good night's sleep allows your body to recuperate, to absorb and assimilate nutrition and to regenerate new cells, while a bad night's sleep is detrimental to your temper, your mental health, your physical health and your concentration at work the following day. A solid bed with a quality supportive mattress is therefore the single most important lifelong investment for your rest, health and longevity.

A Healthy Environment

Your personal environment affects your psychological wellbeing. American researchers have discovered that a chaotic and disorganized environment hinders children's mental development.

A healthy personal environment not only creates pleasant living and working conditions, but it can also minimize undesirable conditions such as allergies caused by dust mites or mould and diseases caused by cross-contamination of bacteria or infestation of pests. Organize your living environment into a simple layout. Don't over-clutter it with ornaments and furniture. Have ample storage areas for keeping any unused items. Apart from being visually spacious and tidy, a simple layout is more accessible and easier for cleaning and dusting. Dust mites feed off dead skin (dust) shedding from humans and pets. Their excrement is the major cause of allergies and asthma. It is therefore crucial to change and wash your bedding often and vacuum your carpets and upholstery weekly.

If you keep pets, you need to vacuum every day. Make sure to bathe and de-flea your pets often and empty their litter to eliminate any unpleasant smells. Install an air filter together with an ionizer in your living area to improve the air quality. Place green houseplants and fresh flowers in your home to beautify your environment. They emit calming energy and oxygen to freshen the air quality. A clean and uncluttered environment gives out positive energy and tranquillity, which is ideal for spiritual cultivation. Cleanliness is next to godliness. Your personal hygiene and the cleanliness of your own environment reflect your willingness and commitment toward the betterment of your spiritual life.

A healthy environment worldwide not only affects the stability of climate, the air we breathe and the water we drink, it also determines long-term global survival. Although a substantial body of evidence has warned about the irreparable damages that we have inflicted upon our environment, our primal self-preservation, greed and arrogance over-ride our common sense and reasoning. We put our short-term personal, economic and national interests first before long-term global survival despite palpable warnings of floods, violent storms, heat waves, tornadoes, coral reef bleaching, drought and forest fire, rising

sea levels and the melting of glaciers and the poles. In spite of entering a pivotal era of global survival, an appreciation of our selfishness and ignorance has yet to be realized. If we abuse our environment continuously at the current rate, the effects will be catastrophic. Experts warn that our planet's stability and its ability to sustain life in the next 20 years will drastically decline by making the following predictions:

• Millions will die from floods, storms, drought, famine, epidemics and war

• Violent storms will hit and reduce shorelines making coastal areas uninhabitable

• Drastic climatic changes including downpours and heavy snowfalls will be followed by flooding

• Agricultural production will fall short significantly because of natural disasters and climatic change

• The human race will fight for survival to access food and water

• Mass migration and the upheaval of millions will be caused by food and water shortages

It is not too late to salvage our environment and avoid further destruction if every individual shares responsibility and takes immediate action. Here are some suggestions:

• Share a vehicle if you travel by car or where possible use public transport, walk or cycle

• Turn off any unused lights

• Turn your heating lower and insulate your house

• Recycle paper and stop buying hardwood products from the rainforests

• Use green alternative energy and empower buildings with energy self-sufficiency

• Plant a few trees

• Buy local green products

• Voice your consumer opinions and join a proactive green organization

• Educate your children about the importance of environmental issues

If everybody gives a little bit more and takes a tiny bit less, we can save our planet without interfering and jeopardizing our economy. Taoists emphasize the importance of understanding universal oneness. Caring for mother earth and looking after our environment is a very positive spiritual step of recognizing the oneness and universality of all beings.

HERBS AND SUPPLEMENTS FOR ETERNAL YOUTH

Chinese herbs have been used for thousands of years in both Chinese cuisine and Chinese medicines for curative functions, promotion of good health and longevity.

Legend tells that the Emperor Shen Nung (3494 BCE) discovered herbal medicine. Shen Nung literally means 'the God of Agriculture' in Chinese. He was considered the father of agriculture because he introduced farming and animal rearing to his subjects. Through farming, he extended his fascination toward the medicinal properties of various plants. Using himself as the guinea pig, through trial and error he established the foundation of Chinese herbal medicine. Shen Nung's medical knowledge passed on from generation to generation orally, as written language was not yet invented. The textual work on Shen Nung's discovery emerged a few hundreds years later, called the *Shen Nung Ben Cao Jing* (*The Book of Shen Nung's Hundred Herbs*). An anonymous author may have edited it by collecting the information from folk medicine and called it this to honour the contribution from the father of Chinese herbal medicine. It is considered

the earliest herbal reference book, with detailed listings of 365 herbs.

Chinese medicine has always been associated with longevity. During the first Qin dynasty (221 –207 BCE), a nobleman, Shui Fu, was asked by the emperor to lead an expedition of some 3,000 young boys and girls to fetch him the herbs of immortality from the Okinawan Islands. The Okinawan and Japanese islands were once thought to be the islands of the Immortals. Knowing their doomed fate if they failed the mission, they never returned to China. Ironically, today Okinawa is considered to be the land of modern Immortals, the world's healthiest and longest-living centenarians. Many of them may have hereditary kinship with the Immortal expedition brigade from China some 2,000 years before. The secrets of their good health and longevity are very similar to those practised by the Taoists.

Ancient Taoist Immortals devised herbal formulations to aid the advancement of Alchemy Meditation. Very elaborate methods of processing extremely complicated formulations were devised, targeting specific organs or decongesting certain meridians. Some of these traditional formulations were prescribed for use at certain times of the day or at certain times of the season according to Five Element Analogy and the calculation of the 'Heavenly Stem and Earthly Branches' calendar. It is very difficult to prove the validity and effectiveness of such practices as some of the ingredients used are highly inaccessible and extremely difficult to process. These ancient methods are no longer practical nor are they compatible with our modern lifestyle.

The formulations used in this book are highly simplified for easy accessibility but it does not in any way diminish their effectiveness. Some of the formulas such as the natural deodorant and the hair tonic are new adaptations. Although they are not originally based on traditional Chinese formulations, they are highly effective. Most of the Chinese herbal ingredients are classified as food grade products and they can be purchased from Chinese supermarkets or western health food stores. Some of the ingredients are also easily accessible from the countryside or your own garden.

Unless you are familiar with botany, it is unwise to pick your own herbs. Although all formulas are safe to use, it is unwise to self-medicate unless you understand the causes of your ailment. For example, a headache can be caused by a cold or a head injury. If you are in doubt consult your physician or your local herbalist. Herbal detoxifiers help to balance Qi and purge toxins from the body, while herbal tonics strengthen Qi harmonization and promote emotional equilibrium. Drinking herbal tonic alone cannot promote good health and longevity especially if you are addicted to social vices such as drinking alcohol or smoking tobacco. You need to incorporate the full spiritual programme of Alchemy Meditation whilse following an unadulterated holistic lifestyle.

Preparation Methods

Traditionally, there are many different ways of treating and preparing herbal ingredients. Decoction, infusion and tincture are the most commonly used methods for both western and Chinese herbal preparation.

These three methods are especially suitable for home users because they do not require any special skills or equipment other than general kitchen utensils and non-metallic earthenware, glassware or enamelware. The ingredients used for these formulas are mostly dry herbs. You should be able to purchase these ingredients easily from Chinese supermarkets, Chinese herbalists or western health food stores. The Chinese herbs are normally sold in clear, vacuum-packed, cellophane packets. Once a packet is opened, the unused herbs should be stored in an airtight container to keep the moisture out.

HOW TO MAKE A DECOCTION

A decoction is an effective way of extracting the herbal ingredients from woody materials, such as the root and bark of the plant. Traditional Chinese decoction vessels are made of earthenware. They can normally be purchased from any Chinese supermarket. Glassware or enamelware is a good substitute for earthenware vessels if you are unable to get a traditional Chinese earthenware herbal vessel.

Put one portion of water to cover up the herbal ingredients in a non-metallic saucepan. Use a medium heat to bring the liquid to the boil. As soon as the liquid is boiling, turn the heat down to simmer the decoction to half of the original volume. More cold water can be added periodically to prolong the simmering time. The longer the simmering time, the more concentrated the concoction that will be produced by the process.

The liquid can then be drunk hot or can be strained into a jar for storing in the refrigerator. For drinking the strained decoction, pour half a cup of the extracted liquid in a cup and top up with boiled water. Brown sugar or honey can be added to take out the bitterness and improve the taste. You can drink the decoction in its neat form if you do not mind the extremely bitter taste.

become. The tincture can then be strained into small bottles for treatment later on.

The 30 ml (1 fl oz) brown bottles with a small rubber drip pump are the ideal type for tincture storage and application. A few drops of tincture can be drunk directly or diluted with water in a cup. Tincture can also be mixed with ointments or lotions for external application.

HOW TO MAKE AN INFUSION

An infusion is a herbal tea. The preparation method is the same as making tea by pouring boiling water into a pot of herbal ingredients to steep and to extract the active ingredients. An infusion can be drunk as a tea-like beverage or it can be used externally as a bathing lotion.

HOW TO MAKE A TINCTURE

A tincture is an effective way of preserving herbal concentrate. Herbal ingredients should be finely chopped or powdered and put into an airtight jar. Pour in sufficient alcohol to submerge the ingredients. Use at least one hundred percent proof alcohol for the preparation. 100 per cent proof means that there is 50 per cent of actual alcohol in the content. The commercial tinctures normally use ethanol. Traditionally, Chinese herbal tinctures use high alcoholic rice wine for the preparation. It is not essential to use Chinese rice wine instead, you can always use vodka, gin, whisky or brandy as the solvent.

Close the lid and let the content stand for at least two weeks. Agitate the jar daily. The longer the tinctures are kept, the more potent they will

Natural Supplements for Long Life

There are a number of natural supplements that can be easily obtained that are essential for health and longevity.

KELP

Kelp is seaweed and can be bought in health food stores in tablet forms. Kelp is rich in iodine and contains selenium and other essential trace minerals. Iodine is essential for secretion of the thyroid hormone, which is necessary for the regulation of oestrogen levels in the body. Iodine, together with selenium, is believed to have an immunological effect against development of cancers, especially breast cancer in women because of its ability to regulate oestrogen levels. Kelp contains complete proteins and antioxidant vitamins A, C and E, which are essential vitamins for combating cellular destruction and premature ageing. Kelp also contains vitamin K, which is essential for synthesizing blood-clotting enzyme prothrombin. Most significantly, kelp contains vitamin B12, which is rarely found in vegetables. Vitamin B12 is fundamental for cellular functions and it is also vital for the metabolism of proteins, fats and carbohydrates. Deficiency of B12 will lead to pernicious anaemia. Kelp is therefore the most vital source of vitamin B12 for all vegetarians and vegans.

BREWER'S YEAST

Brewer's yeast is a miraculous rejuvenating supplement. Apart from B12, brewer's yeast contains the most prolific source of all B vitamins as well as many essential trace elements. These

B vitamins are essential for maintaining healthy skin, digestive tract, heart, eyes and nervous system. Brewer's yeast is an excellent source of iron, chromium, selenium and zinc. Zinc is an important element for the healing process. Zinc, together with vitamin C, works miraculously against allergic symptoms. Zinc is also an essential element for male sexual functions and prevention against prostate cancer. Apart from the values of vitamins and minerals, brewer's yeast is a good source of dietary protein as it contains nearly 50 per cent pure protein.

Brewer's yeast is a natural food supplement and it can be purchased in any health food store in the form of powder or tablets. If you are susceptible to migraine headaches, allergies, eczema and asthma, brewer's yeast may not be suitable for you as you may be allergic to it and also B vitamin supplements.

OILS OF LIFE

Over 2,000 studies have been done on Omega-3 fatty acids revealing that they help to lower cholesterol and blood triglycerides. They also prevent the clotting of blood platelets and so reduce thrombosis and heart attacks. Research has revealed that Omega-3 fatty acids suppress tumour growth in animals. Japanese women have only a third as much breast cancer as American women. Their consumption of mostly fish and soya in their diet may be directly responsible. Scientists at Cardiff University in the UK have recently confirmed the old wife's tale that cod liver oil is an effective treatment for osteoarthritis and it may even have an effect on reversing the destruction of joint cartilage.

Omega-3 fatty acids can be found in natural food sources such as oily fish including salmon, herring, tuna, cod, mackerel and shrimp. If you are a vegetarian or a vegan, you can also obtain Omega-3 fatty acids from flax seed oil, star seed oil, pumpkin seeds, soybean oil and walnuts. Omega-3 supplements can be purchased in most health food stores in bottle and capsule formats. The capsule format is made of gelatine, which may not be suitable for vegetarians and vegans.

LECITHIN

Lecithin is a phospholipid produced by the liver, which is the main component of cell membranes, nerve tissues, semen and brain tissues. It is also an important component for the endocrine glands especially the gonads of both sexes. Lecithin helps to keep your heart healthy by dissolving cholesterol in your arteries, and to keep them staying younger longer. Lecithin contains vitamins D, E and K and essential fatty acids that have the effect of combating cellular oxidation and slowing down ageing. Lecithin can be found in pumpkin seeds, soya beans, walnuts and eggs. Lecithin supplement is sold mostly in granular form in health food stores.

Personal Hygiene for a Youthful Glow

The following recipe suggestions are for tonics, tinctures, deodorants and porridges to keep you healthy from top to toe.

HAIR AND FACE

Your skin is the most obvious indicator of your age. It is your body's first defence against bacterial infection and injury. It also regulates your body temperature and prevents excess water loss. It is an essential excretory organ for toxins and waste produced by your body. To maintain a healthy youthful complexion you need to:

• Avoid direct exposure to the sun or using sun beds. Sun tanning is responsible for 80 per cent of skin ageing. UV rays can cause malignant melanoma, a dangerous skin cancer.

• Stop smoking as it can produce free radicals causing wrinkles and premature ageing.

• Have a low-fat vegetarian diet with a high content of natural antioxidants and natural dietary fibre.

• Drink at least six glasses of clean filtered water daily.

• Make a good habit of moving your bowels daily.

• Perform occasional fasts to detoxify your body.

• Drink herbal tonics to cleanse your body.

• Massage your skin daily with moisturizing lotion/cream.

SKIN TONIC

Dandelion and nettle contain skin-rejuvenating chemicals called retinoids, which can promote production of collagen to make the skin plumper, smoother and less wrinkly. Before moisturizing your skin, use fresh root ginger slices to wipe your face. This will improve the texture of your skin. Avoid wiping too near to your eyes. If you have very sensitive skin, use young (baby) ginger or cucumber instead. Ginger is a natural astringent, which can tighten skin, reduce wrinkles and improve skin texture.

This tonic has very good healing results. It can be applied directly to affected areas such as cuts, boils, bruises or abscesses. You can also mix a few drops of the tincture with an unscented, neutral facial cream or lotion for daily moisturizing.

Ingredients

20 g (¾ oz) marigold (Jin Zian Hua)
20 g (¾ oz) dandelion (Po Gong Ying)
20 g (¾ oz) nettle (Hsieh Tzu Cao)

Method

Prepare as a tincture (see page 109). Remember to let the content stand for at least two weeks and to agitate the jar daily. Use both the leaves and the flowers of the marigold and the whole plant of dandelion and nettle.

EYE WASH

White chrysanthemum can be purchased in most Chinese supermarkets, normally in 150 g (5¼ oz) clear cellophane packets. Make the infusion in a small teapot. Allow it to steep for a while and when the infusion is lukewarm pour it into a bowl. Use some cotton wool to soak up the infusion and bathe the infected eyes. This infusion is ideal for treating conjunctivitis and styes.

Traditionally, white chrysanthemum is used for calming the liver's excessive heat. According to Five Element analogy, the eyes are the external expression of the liver, so the condition of the eyes reflects the health of the liver and vice versa. To make the treatment more effective, you can also drink the white chrysanthemum infusion to aid the treatment internally. This infusion can also be drunk as a health-boosting tonic both for the eyes and for balancing liver Qi.

Ingredients

White chrysanthemum (Bai Ju Hua),
  a small handful

Method

Prepare as an infusion (see page 109). Remember that this is made as you would normally make tea.

HAIR TONIC

It is natural to lose approximately 100 hairs each day. Baldness in men is predetermined by their genetic disposition. Abnormal hair loss for women is normally due to hormonal imbalance. This formula does not offer any miracle regrowth of hair but it can strengthen hair follicles and prolong the hair growing cycle. All of these ingredients work together to stimulate the circulation of blood to the area.

Apply a few drops of the tincture to your scalp and massage daily. You can also mix the tincture with your shampoo and conditioner to strengthen the treatment. Other factors that determine healthy hair growth are hygiene, nutrition, exercise and living a stress-free life. Tofu, beans, bean sprouts, mushrooms, seeds, grains, seaweed and broccoli are good sources of nutrition for healthy hair growth. In Chinese medicine, strong kidney energy is reflected by the strength of hair growth. Therefore, taking ginseng tonic for men or dong quai tonic for women together with performing daily back massage (Mo Bei) on the kidneys can harmonize kidney Qi and strengthen hair growth.

Ingredients

1 part onion (Yang Tsung), finely chopped
1 part nettle (Hsieh Tzu Cao)
3 teaspoons sage (Shu Wei Cao)
3 teaspoons rosemary (Mi Die Xiang)
½ teaspoon cayenne pepper (Hong Chiao)

Method

Prepare as a tincture for external use only (see page 109). It should stand for at least two weeks and the jar must be shaken daily.

COLONIC HYGIENE

The United Kingdom is one of the most constipated nations in the world. It is estimated that one in 14 people in the United Kingdom has constipation at any one time, and one in ten of those with the condition is constipated on a regular basis. If you experience chronic constipation, you are most likely to have bad breath, eruptive skin, frequent migraines and abdominal pain as the toxins in your faeces are reabsorbed into your circulatory system. It may even develop into more serious disorders, such as haemorrhoids, irritable bowel syndrome, colitis, diverticulitis, depression, Parkinson's disease, multiple sclerosis and colon cancer. Colon cancer (bowel cancer) is killing around 20,000 people a year in the UK. Colon cancer is the third most common type of cancer in the USA and it is responsible for more than 56,000 deaths a year. A diet low in dietary fibre, high in saturated fats and a disproportionate amount of meat, as well as overcooked, burned and smoked food, are the major contributing factors of this deadly disease. A healthy colon is therefore an important key to good health and longevity.

If you suffer from constipation, here are the steps that you need to take to eliminate and correct the problem.

• Eat a diet with little or no meat and high in natural dietary fibre, preferably a vegetarian diet with a high intake of green vegetables and fruits. Do not confuse eating breakfast cereal or bran as a substitute for natural dietary fibre. They are processed foods, which are high in acrylamide and other additives and may cause food intolerance and other problems.

• Drink six to eight glasses of clean filtered water or green tea a day.

• Avoid eating refined sugar and carbohydrates, fried food, unnatural additives and excessive saturated fats.

• Make a habit of moving your bowels daily.

• Avoid using commercial laxatives as they can reduce or disable the natural peristaltic movements of the intestines.

• Exercise daily and massage your abdomen daily.

• Eat natural yoghurt or acidophilus/bifidus supplements.

• Use a natural laxative remedy, see right.

• Drink Chinese detoxifying herbal tea. Chinese medicine looks upon chronic constipation as excessive heat in the colon. Drinking herbal tea, which is viewed traditionally as having a cool nature, can correct the problem.

CONSTIPATION CURE

This is one of my favourite formulas because the recipe is also traditionally used as a Chinese dessert. Black sesame seeds and slab cane sugar can be bought from most Chinese supermarkets.

For the treatment of constipation, eat three to four bowls of hot sesame porridge. It should normally work within a few hours. This formula has to be the most natural, tastiest and effective laxative I have ever known.

Ingredients

200 g (7 oz) black sesame seeds (Hei Chih Ma)
80 g (3 oz) long grain rice (Bai Mi)
1 or 2 slabs cane sugar (Pein Tang)

Method

Soak the sesame seeds and rice in a bowl of water for at least 12 hours. Use a food processor or a blender to grind the sesame seed mixture to a very fine paste.

Half-fill a saucepan with cold water and pour the paste into the saucepan gradually while stirring. Continue to stir the mixture and gently simmer it under a low heat until it reaches a porridge consistency. You might need to add more water to thin the paste down as it is simmering. It is entirely up to you to make the consistency of the porridge thicker or thinner. You can put in a slab of cane sugar to taste. If you make the porridge thick, you can also set it inside a jelly mould in the fridge and eat it later as a cold dessert.

STOMACH TONIC FOR SICKNESS AND STOMACH ULCERS 1

This formula is ideal for treating digestive disorders such as stomach ulcers, sickness, including morning sickness for expectant mothers, and hyperacidity. The root ginger can be chopped or bruised for boiling. Small amounts of decoction should be sipped as required. In Chinese medical terms, symptoms such as stomach ulcers and hyperacidity are coldness in the stomach. The warm nature of ginger has the effect of restoring the balance. The decoction is also effective at expelling excessive wind, which can induce a lot of burping as a result of the treatment.

You can also make a tincture by soaking the ginger, without the sugar, in alcohol. Two to three drops of the tincture can be taken as required. Ginger tincture is a good preventive remedy for travel sickness.

Ingredients

60 g (2 oz) root ginger (Jaing)
Slab cane sugar (Pein Tang),
    small amount to half slab

Method

Prepare as a decoction or a tincture (see pages 108 and 109).

STOMACH TONIC FOR SICKNESS AND STOMACH ULCERS 2

This formula is effective for treating advanced stomach ulcers. Yarrow is traditionally used for stopping bleeding and amenorrhoea (menstruation difficulties). Yarrow is therefore not suitable for pregnant women.

One cup of concentrated decoction can be sipped slowly every day until symptoms subside. Alternatively, take three to five drops of the tincture two times a day.

Ingredients

30 g (1 oz) yarrow (I Chi Kao)
60 g (2 oz) root ginger (Jaing)

Method

Prepare as a decoction or a tincture (see pages 108 and 109).

NATURAL DEODORANT

Recent research suggests that daily use of aerosols such as deodorants and air fresheners is associated with a 30 per cent increase in infantile diarrhoea, and it also affects a mother's health. Commercial deodorant contains aluminium chloride, a narcotic, which can irritate the skin and its long-term harmful effects are unknown. Several common components are also well-known carcinogenic agents, which may have immediate and long-term toxic effects on vital organs.

It is a common misconception that body odour comes from body sweat. In fact, perspiration itself is rather odourless. The offensive odour is actually created by bacteria, which can flourish in a warm and moist environment, such as your armpits and feet. Bacteria cannot grow in an alkaline condition, therefore, if you alter the pH balance of their potential culturing environment, you will also eliminate the offensive odour caused by the bacterial growth. Baking powder, sometimes sold under the name of sodium bicarbonate, is the main active ingredient for the natural deodorant inhibiting bacterial growth.

This deodorant is for external use only.

Ingredients

½ teaspoon baking powder (sodium bicarbonate)
½ teaspoon talcum powder
Scented body cream, small amount (optional)

Method

Mix the baking powder and talcum powder together. If you pre-mix the powder in bulk quantity, store it in a talcum-powder dispenser in a dry place to avoid caking.

To use, sprinkle the powder generously onto your feet or under your armpits. You can apply body cream under your armpits to enhance the adhesion of the powder.

DEODORANT FOR YOUR ARMPITS

Mix half a teaspoonful of baking powder with your favourite body cream and apply the mixture to your armpits. Your favourite body cream acts as a binder for the baking powder and introduces a pleasant smell to your natural deodorant.

DEODORANT FOR YOUR FEET AND FOOTWEAR

Mix one portion of baking powder with one portion of talcum powder and sprinkle onto your feet and inside your shoes. This will eliminate any odour developing from your feet or inside the footwear, which is often made of synthetic materials.

DEODORANT FOR THE CARPET

You can also use the above formula to deodorize your carpet. Sprinkle the mixture onto your carpet and leave it overnight before vacuuming it thoroughly the next day.

Herbal Remedies for Common Ailments

The following recipes are formulas to treat everyday problems. I have included decoctions for common ailments such as coughs, colds and headaches and for detoxifying.

COUGH REMEDY

Both bitter almond and sweet almond can be bought from Chinese supermarkets. They are often labelled as northern and southern almonds. Almond, especially bitter almond, contains hydrocyanic acid, which is slightly poisonous when eaten raw. However, hydrocyanic acid is also susceptible to hydrolysis at higher temperatures, therefore using almonds in a decoction is perfectly safe. Northern and southern almonds are frequently used together to resolve phlegm and allay coughs.

To prepare sweet almond and bitter almond, put the kernels in a bowl of hot water and soak them for five minutes. Then peel off the loose brown skin from the kernels. Sugar cane can be bought from Asian supermarkets. Some Chinese supermarkets also sell them in a dehydrated format. To prepare sugar cane, chop it up into sections, about 5 cm (2 in) long, and then cut them into slices. Congongrass rhizome is sometimes sold together with dehydrated sugar cane. It is used for dispelling heat (fever), calming coughs and maintaining liquid balance. The carrot is a natural calmative. It is added to soothe the lungs, calm coughs and dispel heat (fever). This formula is very effective for calming coughs caused by cold, flu and asthma.

Ingredients

10–15 kernels bitter almond
   (Nan Hsing Jen)
10–15 kernels sweet almond
   (Bei Hsing Jen)
1 stick suger cane
Congongrass rhizome
   (Mao Ken) 30 g (1 oz)
1 large carrot

Method

Prepare as a decoction (see page 108).

SORE THROAT AND COLD REMEDY

Apart from using it as a condiment for cooking and baking, traditionally clove (especially clove oil) is used to stop toothache. Clove has the properties of anodyne, antiemetic and antiseptic; therefore, clove itself is an excellent herb for a bacterial type of throat infection. Honey has long been recognized for its natural soothing, calming quality and traditionally honey and lemon are used for alleviating cold symptoms. This formula is also excellent for sore throats caused by hay fever. Root ginger can be added if you feel nausea or if your sore throat is caused by cold and flu symptoms. Add mandarin peel to discharge phlegm. The decoction can be drunk liberally during the affected period.

Ingredients

5–10 cloves (Ding Xiang)
1 tablespoon honey
½ lemon, sliced
2–3 slices root ginger (Jaing) (optional)
small pieces mandarin peel (Chen Pi) (optional)

Method

Prepare as a decoction (see page 108).

HEADACHE, FEVER, FLU AND CONGESTION

Dandelion is effective for clearing fevers and allaying congestion. Elder is traditionally used for setting fractured bones. Its excellent properties include stimulating circulation and alleviating pain. Peppermint promotes perspiration and reduces fevers. Yarrow is excellent for treating colds, flu and fevers, promoting perspiration in fevers, inducing menstruation and healing fibroid tumours. Pregnant women should omit Yarrow in this formula. Mandarin peel is an expectorant, which helps to discharge mucus and phlegm.

Prepare a fresh decoction and sip it hot slowly. Honey can be added to take away the bitterness and strengthen the sedative effects.

Ingredients

1 part dandelion (Po Gong Ying)
1 part elder (Chieh Ku Mu)
1 part peppermint (Bo He)
1 part yarrow, *Achillea sibirica ledeb* (I Chi Kao)
2–4 slices root ginger (Jaing)
small pieces of mandarin peel
   (Chen Pi) (optional)
Honey (optional)

Method

Prepare as a decoction (see page 108).

Qi Strengthening

Qi strengthening must work in two stages, purging and nourishing. Firstly, use the Blood purifier/detoxifer to purge toxins and bad Qi, the excessive Qi that causes imbalance and Qi stagnation in the body.

For example, too much liver Qi (wood) subjugates spleen Qi (earth) that causes symptoms of headache, loss of appetite or chest discomfort. Herbal detoxification works more effectively during a fasting period. Choose one of the formulas below or combine both formulas for doubling the strength of the purge. Once the bad Qi and toxins are eliminated, take Ginseng tonic for men or Dong Quai tonic for women to nourish the body and strengthen Qi harmony.

BLOOD PURIFIER/DETOXIFIER 1

This formula is to be prepared as a concentrated decoction and can be diluted and drunk liberally, especially during fasting periods. This formula is ideal for blood purification, to improve circulation, for detoxification, to improve Qi flow and to boost your body's immunity against colds, flu and allergies. These herbs are classified as cool in nature in Chinese medicine and the formula is normally known as cool tea. Therefore, this formula is also ideal for treating heat-natured diseases, such as fever, inflammations, rheumatic swellings, haemorrhoids and constipation. All heal and honeysuckle are also widely used by western herbalists. All heal, also known as self heal, as the name suggests is an excellent healing herb. Traditionally, the infusion of all heal is used for bathing and cleaning wounds. Finally, licorice root is used for dispelling heat, detoxification and for strengthening spleen and stomach functions.

Ingredients

1 part all heal (Ku Cao)
1 part honeysuckle (Jin Yin Hua)
1 part white chrysanthemum (Bai Ju Hua)
3–4 slices licorice root
   (Gan Cao) (optional)

Method

Prepare as a decoction (see page 108).

BLOOD PURIFIER/DETOXIFIER 2

If you do not have access to any Chinese supermarkets in your locality, this is another excellent substitute formula as these herbs are widely available in the wild. You may also find them growing in your own back garden, but you may have dug them up, considering them weeds. These herbs can also be bought in most western health food stores. If you pick your own fresh herbs, use the whole plant including the root. Dandelion is diuretic, therefore drinking this decoction will induce a constant need to go to the toilet. As with the first formula, these herbs are also classified as cool in nature and can eliminate bad hot Qi from the body. Chinese herbalists frequently use dandelion for treating swelling and tumours. Research studies conducted in China, Japan and Korea have revealed the positive effect of using dandelion to treat tumours and cancer.

Recent studies in the USA showed that dandelion and nettle contain vitamin A related chemicals called retinoids that may offer protection against breast cancer. Thistle is a cholagogue, an agent for increasing bile secretion into the intestines. Western herbalists traditionally use thistle to treat liver disease. Recent research suggests that thistle may help to treat some liver diseases including hepatitis and cirrhosis and may have a preventive property of inhibiting prostate carcinoma and colon cancer growth. Using these herbs helps anti-ageing and has positive preventive effects on diseases.

Ingredients

1 part thistle (Hsiao Chi)
1 part dandelion (Po Gong Ying)
1 part nettle (Hsieh Tzu Cao)
3–4 slices licorice root (Gan Cao)

Method

Prepare as a decoction (see page 108).

Tonics for Sexual Vitality

In this section I have prescribed herbs to improve general wellbeing and tonics to help women with menstruation problems and to assist men with impotence.

SEXUAL VITALITY FOR MEN

Ginseng, the herb of longevity, has long been prescribed by Chinese physicians for its anti-ageing powers. The herb is known to be an effective cure for irritability, fatigue and other neurasthenic troubles. It also strengthens the immune system, improves eyesight, vitalizes mental faculties and builds physical strength. Recent studies have confirmed ginseng's healthful qualities. Ginseng:

- Suppresses the cellular destruction of free radicals

- Delivers chemical compounds such as phenol and maltol that have anti-stress and anti-ageing effects

- Activates the body's natural defences against tumours and cancer cells

- Improves lipid metabolism and prevents arteriosclerosis and hypertension

- Suppresses gastric ulcer formation and improves blood circulation in the gastric mucous membrane

- Enhances brain activity and maintains psychological stability

Ginseng's principal fame, however, is as a cure for impotence and as a potent aphrodisiac. It strengthens the libido and enhances penile erectile functions in men. Maintaining sexual vitality is certainly an important part of staying young. But there is a common misunderstanding concerning the Taoist way of preserving sexual vitality. Some Taoist texts suggest that, in order to prolong life, men should withhold ejaculation during intercourse. The basis of this belief is that semen was equated with Jing, the Essence of Life. It was thought that if men withheld their semen it could be reabsorbed into the body to nourish the brain.

However, the practice of withholding semen, called 'Killing the White Tiger', is not actually a longevity practice. It probably arose in

ancient China as a way of prolonging men's sexual pleasure and increasing their sexual conquests. At the time, China was a male-dominated feudalistic society, in which polygamy was an acceptable social norm. In today's world, the practice is foolish, unscientific and superstitious.

Withholding ejaculation violates the fundamental Taoist principle of the balance of duality. As *Tao Te Jing*, puts it: 'Be empty and you will become filled.' In other words, when semen is ejaculated, more semen will be generated. It is nature's intention to accomplish this natural cycle. Taoist ways are natural ways: Wu Wei is the natural Tao. The best way to rejuvenate your sexual health is to practice the Alchemy Meditation and the complementary exercises, especially the Dan Tien massage (Mo Dan Tien), the back massage (Mo Bei) and the teeth clenching (Kou Chi) exercise. These ancient practices greatly increase sexual vitality.

Taking natural supplements of vitamin C, vitamin E, zinc and lecithin and eating pumpkin seeds can enhance sexual vitality and guard against prostate cancer. You can also use the natural herbal tonic on the right. It gets its potency from Korean red ginseng (Kao Li Shen), with its many anti-ageing qualities. The tonic also helps to rejuvenate the male reproductive system and prolong the healthy regeneration of semen and sexual hormones.

GINSENG TONIC FOR MEN

You can buy these ingredients in most Chinese supermarkets and herb shops. Hong Zao, Huai Shan and Gou Qi Zi are often packaged together as nourishing soup ingredients. These herbs have a benevolent effect on the digestive system and aid the absorption and assimilation of ginseng. Huai Shan and Gou Qi Zi are also traditionally used for treating sexual disorders such as impotence. Ginger can be added to this formula to warm the stomach and strengthen the digestive system. The decoction is best drunk hot like soup. The herbal ingredients can also be eaten.

Ingredients

50–60 g (1¾–2 oz) Korean red ginseng
  (Kao Li Shen)
3 or 4 dates or jujube
  (Hong Zao or Da Zao)
5–6 pieces potato yam
  (Huai Shan)
5–10 g (⅕–⅓ oz) wolfberry
  (Gou Qi Zi)
2–3 slices root ginger (Jaing) (optional)

Method

Prepare as a decoction (see page 108).

SEXUAL VITALITY FOR WOMEN

A woman's sexual cycle is pre-determined by nature's time clock. From puberty to menopause, the pituitary gland regulates the ovaries to produce oestrogen and progesterone. These hormones prepare women for conception and motherhood by alternating ovulation and menstruation cycles. The hormonal balance has a profound effect on a woman's physical and emotional wellbeing throughout her lifetime.

Dong Quai (*Angelica sinensis*) is also phonetically known as Tang Kuei or Dong Gui. The root of the plant has been used in the treatment of female menstrual problems in China, Japan and Korea for thousands of years. Dong Quai is reputed as a tonic and its popularity is only second to ginseng. Some people even call it the women's ginseng. It is a calmative and a blood tonic. It is commonly used for treating a wide range of women's gynaecological complaints including:

• Regulating menstrual irregularity

• Easing period pain and ensuring a healthy pregnancy and easy delivery

• Eliminating discomfort of pre-menstrual syndrome

• Helping women resume normal menstruation after they come off the pill

Dong Quai has always been used for boosting circulation, dispersing bruises and as a treatment for insomnia for both sexes. Recent scientific studies corroborate that Dong Quai can promote good health and longevity as it has the ability to:

• Dilate coronary vessels and increase coronary blood flow which in turn lowers the blood pressure and slows down the heart rate and the respiratory rate

• Reduce atherosclerosis formation

• Improve body immunity as it has anti-inflammatory and anti-bacterial effects

• Lower blood cholesterol levels in experimental animals and prolong life span

Dong Quai Tonic has a profound effect on women's sexual health. It is equally important to conduct a holistic lifestyle. To maintain sexual vitality and emotional equilibrium, you need to:

• Have a well-balanced diet (preferably a vegetarian diet) with little meat and lots of fruits and vegetables, especially green vegetables. A diet high in animal protein encourages your body to excrete more calcium, oxalate and uric acid, causing formation of urinary tract stones and calcium loss. Calcium loss is the major factor in osteoporosis during menopause.

- Drink carrot juice to increase vitamin A intake. Vitamin A can reduce pre-menstrual syndrome.

- Eat lots of grains, seeds, nuts, beans and tofu to boost the intake of magnesium, zinc, lecithin and B D, E and K vitamins. Tofu contains flavonoids and polyphenols, which have the ability to slow down bone loss, counteracting hormone-related cancers and reducing hot flushes during menopause.

- Take natural supplements: kelp, brewer's yeast, omega-3 oils. Omega-3 oils prevent development of breast cancer and relieve symptoms of dysmenorrhoea.

- Cutting out coffee, refined sugar and refined carbohydrates can minimize mood swings, tender breasts and migraines before and during menstruation.

- Practising Alchemy Meditation and complementary exercises such as massaging the Dan Tien and the kidney areas can rejuvenate and revitalize the sexual sphere. Toning the PC muscle with the teeth clenching exercise (Kou Chi) will greatly enhance enjoyment of sex and prevent a prolapsed uterus at an advanced age.

DONG QUAI TONIC FOR WOMEN

Apart from Dong Quai and peony root, all the other ingredients are the same as the tonic for men. Add peony root for a curative effect if you suffer from irregular or heavy menstruation. Dong Quai tonic has powerful effects on balancing Qi and blood as well as promoting sexual vitality, fertility and longevity. This decoction is best drunk hot like soup and the herbal ingredients can also be eaten.

Ingredients

10–12 slices angelica (Dong Quai)
½ root Korean red ginseng
   (Kao Li Shen)
3 or 4 dates or jujube
   (Hong Zao or Da Zao)
5–6 pieces potato yam
   (Huai Shan)
5–10 g (⅕–⅓ oz) wolfberry
   (Gou Qi Zi)
2–3 slices root ginger
   (Jaing) (optional)
5–6 pieces peony root (Bai Shao) (optional)

Method

Prepare as a decoction (see page 108).

CULTIVATING SPIRITUAL IMMORTALITY

What attracted you to this book in the first place? Perhaps you were fascinated by the concepts of good health, rejuvenation, longevity and Immortality. Maybe you are a student of esoteric arts who is seeking a deeper understanding about arcane wisdom? Or perhaps you are merely looking for ideas to transform your life or new directions to motivate you?

Whatever the reasons that inspired you to read this book, I believe there is an element of curiosity, a yearning for knowledge and an aspiration for change.

Indeed good health, longevity and spiritual happiness can really be achieved if you prepare to transform your life and follow the Taoist Immortal Programme. How are you doing so far? Do you feel inspired and eager to practise the meditation and to try out all the healthy living paradigms to revolutionize your life? Or maybe you feel overwhelmed by the enormous volume of information and you don't know where to begin? I suspect that you may feel both. Now you may well ask, 'What should I do next?' or 'How do I begin?'

You have already begun on a very special life-changing journey by reading this book. This is a journey of energy transformation, which will rejuvenate your body, broaden your mind and illuminate your spirit – a passage of life modification which is positive, happy, radiant, caring, non-judgemental, holistic, creative, compassionate and contributory. It is a voyage of liberation which will free you from stress, worry, ill health, selfishness, negative emotions and fear of death. Congratulations for making such a life-changing decision and welcome aboard!

Making changes in life may appear to be daunting at the beginning, unless you have a clear strategy for structuring the changes. You do not have to follow every little step written within this book. It is better to pick and choose the materials and to customize a programme to suit your personal circumstances. See what is most lacking in your life, diet, exercise or personal environment. Tackling your shortcomings is normally the best starting point to initiate change. Every journey begins with the first step. Recognizing your shortcomings is a big leap forward in your life-changing experience. Once you have identified your starting point, the action plan (see right) shows how you can follow up with the programme.

For every little change you are making, you are taking a positive step forward for the betterment of your life. Remember, do it in stages, study in small chunks and go over the book again and again to utilize the information. Soon you will find yourself assimilating the techniques and integrating the disciplines routinely into your everyday life. You will then live as a physically healthy, mentally balanced and spiritually awakened modern Taoist. When your life is transformed you will be stepping onto the positive pathway toward Immortality.

DRAW UP AN ACTION PLAN

- Set goals of what you want to achieve within a framework of time. Don't be over-ambitious with your plan and be realistic about what you can achieve. Once you have set your goals, you can see things with more clarity. Also, when you have written down your goals, you have made a symbolic pact with yourself.

- Read a small section of this book daily and work according to your 'to do list'. Go over the section again and again in small chunks until you can fully understand the meaning.

- Practise the techniques over and over again.

- Pick one subject at a time, maybe on diet, personal hygiene, personal environment or exercises, and make small changes in small steps daily or weekly until you have totally integrated the changes as part of your life.

- Write a weekly diary on the subjects on which you have taken action, to monitor your personal progress.

Emotional Wellbeing

People age before their time in our modern society. It is curious that people are compelled to behave in certain ways and conform to certain social expectations as soon as they are retired.

Many people resign their final years to resting, watching unproductive TV programmes or playing domino and bingo games all day. Their social group is confined to a small circle of retired pensioners who can only talk about old times or gossip about their neighbours' trivial matters.

A CREATIVE LIFE

The truth is that you are as old as you feel. Your own mental attitude, your willingness to meet new friends, to take on new challenges, to learn a new subject or to actively engage in a creative project can prolong your life span. While some people say that they are too old for any of these activities, or too old to mix with young people, they unconsciously tell themselves that they want to be excluded from society as they do not want to go on living any longer. Similar to our muscles and skeleton, the more we exercise and flex our brain, the stronger and the better developed it will become to service us. It is very simple: be engaging and participate in new interests, meet new friends and take on new challenges so as to keep your life refreshed and enriched. Don't allow your advancing years to be an excuse to hinder you from meeting friends of all age groups and enjoying a productive and creative life. Remember, your brain also governs all your physical activities; therefore, your attitudes to

ageing can affect you psychologically and physically. Creative projects are therefore important to stimulate your grey matter and to keep your mind young, active and alert. Instead of watching television all day, join a club or a community college, mix with young people and try out a new hobby like electronics and radio, computing and internet technology, drama and operatics, alternative therapies and healing arts or plumbing and electrical maintenance. Take on new challenges, such as studying for a degree, building a model plane, renovating a house or learning to play a new musical instrument. You can also join a group that involves community activities, such as a carnival organizing committee, a charity to raise funds for the developing world, an association for animal protection or a group for local projects. Your community spirit, social involvement, friendship and the sense of doing good will also have a very positive impact on your psychological and mental health. You don't need to wait till you are retired to take on a new hobby or to take on a new creative project. If you can make your life fun, productive and creative, all the positive energies will be in place to shape a happier and healthier life.

Continuous, constructive and creative thinking can transform negative emotions into positive achievements. When you take on new challenges, you will require a full focus of mental concentration and a positive attitude to tackle the problem head on. In this heightened positive mental attitude, you will become more in tune with your creative inner self. Eventually, your sense of accomplishment will manifest as a sense of deep spiritual contentment and happiness. A creative life is essential to enhance your physical, psychological and mental health. A creative life will also encourage you to be active, to have a positive attitude to everything and to generate continuous new aspirations to extend your life to its full potential.

THE MIRACLE OF MUSIC

Music and sound can influence human emotions. Since the era of the silent movies filmmakers have understood the power of using music and sound effects to sway the audience's emotions and to incite joy, fear or anger according to the dramatic sequence of the movie. Science has long known that music and harmonious sounds are panaceas to negative emotions. Sound therapy and music therapy are becoming increasingly recognized for their true values.

People do have a positive response to the vibrations of sound, through the rhythm and its resonance. If you were subjected to the hammering noise of a neighbour's home-improvement project all day, your mood would undoubtedly become anxious, angry and stressful. On the contrary, if you were listening to a piece of harmonious classical music, the sympathetic resonance would vibrate through your body and create a sense of harmony to make you feel good, joyful and elated.

Both Chinese Taoists and Indian yogis have used the science of sound to gain health and harmony for thousands of years. Taoists long recognized the relationship between emotions, organs and sounds in the Five Element synthesis.

FIVE ELEMENT SYNTHESIS

Element	Organ	Emotion	Response
Wood	Liver/Gall Bladder	Anger	Shout
Fire	Heart/Small Intestine	Joy	Laugh
Earth	Spleen/Stomach	Obsession	Sing
Metal	Lung/Large Intestine	Sadness	Wail
Water	Kidney/Bladder	Fear	Sigh

Taoists further developed the six healing
sounds, Qi Gong, using sound to harmonize the
emotions and the internal organs. Similarly,
Hindus use mantra yoga for healing and accessing
higher consciousness. Other faiths such as
Christianity and Islam also use psalms and chants
for their prayers and healing purposes. In fact, if
you can sing a happy song every day, you can
bring enormous benefits to your physical,
psychological and mental wellbeing. Singing is an
outlet of your emotional expression. Sing out
loud and sing with all your emotion and you will
be surprised how much a song can uplift your
spirit. If you can play an instrument, play it to
accompany your singing. Playing an instrument

would be considered a double bonus to the healing energy. The harmonics, the resonance, the creative inspiration and the sense of accomplishment, together with the artistic expression, can levitate your mood and bring out the deepest joyous emotions.

Learn to play a musical instrument if you have not played any instruments previously. You don't need to be a concert performer to enjoy the creativity, harmony and health benefits of playing a musical instrument. Singing and playing musical instruments are enjoyable ways of expressing yourself creatively – there is no right or wrong way to do it. Do sway your body, clap your hands or tap your feet while you are singing. Try to synchronize your movements, claps and taps with the rhythm, syncopation and dynamics of the piece to create a crescendo of expression. Allow your body, your soul and your whole being to sing, resonate, immerse and harmonize with the music you are making. Singing, dancing and making music are the most natural things to do when we want to express our happiness or to share celebratory occasions. Do join a local voice group, a choir, an operatic society or a dance group to expand your social circle and to enrich a musical and creative life. Make a happy, celebratory life and let your soul bathe in the harmonious resonance of songs, dance, movement, expression, music and laughter.

FRIENDS AND FAMILY

One of the Okinawan centenarians' secrets of good health and longevity is having an excellent support system both religiously and socially. Their community network, friendship, social support and spirituality enhance their optimism and their abilities to deal with stress and to cope with death. As Maslow (1968) suggested, one of man's hierarchy of needs is the need for love and a sense of belonging. Everybody needs somebody. Nobody can live in a modern world without any human interaction, love and support unless you are a castaway on a desert island like Robinson Crusoe, and even he found his Man Friday.

Indeed friends and family can elevate your mood, give you love and support if your relationship with them is built upon mutual trust, mutual respect, mutual growth and unconditional love. They can also depress you, sadden you and make you feel alone and isolated if the relationship is built upon mistrust, rivalry, jealousy and hatred. George Burns once said: 'Happiness is having a large, loving, caring, close-knit family in another city.' Behind the funny remark rings a truth that we all need care, love and support as long as we can also have our independence. We all need our personal space for reflection and personal growth no matter how intimate the relationship we have with our loved ones or how strong the friendship with our buddies. In our western society, we certainly require a very large personal space as George Burns perceptively and humorously put it.

To build a positive relationship with your friends and family, you must learn to value them for what they are. No relationship is a perfect relationship. You can choose your friends but you cannot choose your family. It takes a lot of give and take to harmonize among all family members. Charity begins at home. You must give your love for the sake of love as a pure gift from the heart. You must not stifle your loved ones but recognize instead their need for personal space for growth and reflection. You should not demand anything in return; your love should be unconditional and free from hidden agendas. Lastly, you should not seek to claim ownership of your relationship with them; you need to recognize their personal freedom and free will and not seek to treat them as your personal possessions. Mutual respect must first come from your respect towards others. A friend in need is a friend indeed. A true friend can confide in you, encourage you, support you and console you when you most require it. A bad friend can misguide you, exploit you and ruin you. Value good friendship and always be mindful to return a kindness or a good deed.

When sitting quietly, reflect upon your own faults. When speaking with friends do not discuss the rights and wrongs of others. Your internal harmony affects your external environment and the people you associate with. I have treated some people who went into chronic depression after their children left home. As a Taoist, you must understand that nothing is eternal and all things are constantly transforming. If you give more, demand less and learn to let go, you will not have sadness during parting or when relationships break up. If there is misunderstanding, be the first person to make peace. Once again, let go of your pride and your instinct of winning. Nobody wins in an argument when disharmony prevails.

A good and loving relationship can fulfill your life emotionally and spiritually. A bad relationship can destroy families, be detrimental to your health and damage your children. Therefore, when you look for love and long-term partnership, don't just go with the impulse of physical and sexual attraction alone. Look into the innate qualities of kindness, friendship, flexibility and the ability to give, care and share. Explore the mutuality of interests, spiritual inspirations, values, a sense of humour, intelligence and education. Look to see if you can understand each other intellectually and spiritually. Establish whether you can communicate at all levels and at the same time complement each other with your strengths and weaknesses. A soulmate can be found but a really good relationship requires long-term trust-building, communication, unconditional love, mutual respect and collaboration.

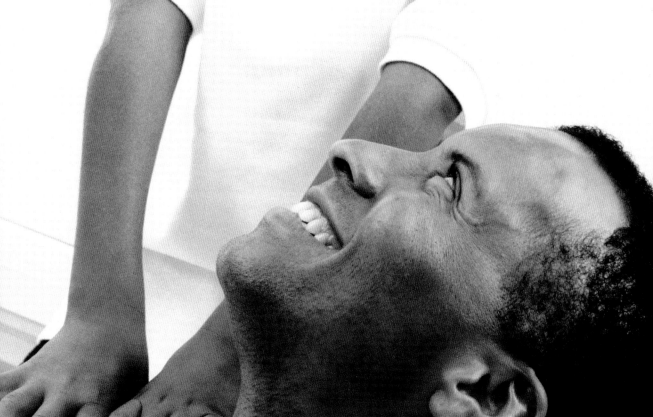

THE GIFT OF A SMILE

Yes, smile, my friend. As I stated briefly (on page 32), smiling is your first step to attain profound spiritual happiness, good health and longevity. You can be happy for the sake of feeling happy and you can be sad for the sake of wanting to feel sad. A lot of people become depressed as a result of permanently adopting a habitual frown and a fear reflex posture. When you are happy, sad, angry or anxious, you always express these emotions with your facial expression. Your facial expression will then signal to your body and your mind to respond to these emotions. If you frown, the frowning tells your brain that you are feeling sad or worried. Your brain will reaffirm your emotional request with a fear reflex by instructing your body to raise your shoulders, slump your chest and retract your neck. Tension will then build up in your neck, shoulders and back, making you feel even more anxious, worried and depressed. The more you are anxious and depressed, the more your fear reflex will tense up your muscles. The frown and the muscular tension will become habitual actions and a vicious cycle of psychosomatic torment. This is why some people find it very hard to come out of a depression. On the contrary, if you smile, you will relax your facial muscles. Your physical relaxation signals to your brain to translate it as contentment and happiness. Your brain will then instruct your body to relax and maintain a positive and upright posture.

If you greet someone with a smile or a frown, they will mirror your emotions involuntarily. Your emotions do not just affect your own health and your psychosomatic balance, but they also influence your external environment as well as the people that you associate with. Imagine that your boss walks into the office with a frown. What will your reaction be? You will most likely be worried that something has gone wrong or that your boss will be in a bad mood for the rest of the day. You will mirror your boss's emotion in the first instant and follow by expressing your worry with a frown. Your brain will then signal to your body to reflect that emotion by raising your shoulders and retracting your neck. Then, during the rest of the day, the habitual frowning, together with the tension in your neck, shoulders and

back, will instruct your brain to further translate these signals as more worry and stress. When you greet your clients, no matter how hard you try, you will not be able to shake off your negative emotions. You will give them a sad smile and communicate with an uneasy, stressful body language. What kind of signals are you giving to your clients? Surely, using unconstructive emotions and negative body language is not a positive way to build a good business relationship.

As your unconscious mind exerts direct control over your facial muscles and expresses your emotions, when you smile you tell your unconscious mind that you are happy, tranquil, positive, upbeat, inspired, grateful and spiritually contented. Your body will instantly become relaxed and upright. The energy emanating from your body will become positive, open, sincere and vibrant. When you smile, the whole world will smile along with you. Remember, when you smile, you are relaxing your facial muscles, signalling to your body to relax and your mind to become tranquil. You are also indicating to others that you are friendly, approachable, confident, trustworthy and welcoming. Smiling is good for building relationships and reserving energy. Your harmony within yourself and your surroundings allows you to become more in tune with your spiritual nature. So, if you want to access the key to true spiritual happiness, do this simple facial exercise: smile, smile, smile.

Spiritual Wellbeing: Healthy Body, Healthy Mind

In addition to the Alchemy Meditation and the complementary exercises, other Taoist arts such as Tai Chi and Qi Gong have great benefits for promoting good health and longevity. Tai Chi and Qi Gong are total exercises for body, mind and spirit.

The slow regulation of breathing together with meditative concentration helps to restore vitality, de-stress the body and focus the mind. You learn to use your body as a child would, moving in a natural, soft and graceful manner, which in turn improves your balance and corrects your posture. Meditative exercises are renowned for improving conditions such as cardiovascular, respiratory and digestive disorders, neurasthenia, hypertension and stress. They also have remarkable effects on the mind, influencing it in terms of concentration, memory retention, positive thinking and confidence.

Tai Chi is a martial art and it is practised widely in China and many South East Asian countries as a healing art form because of its gentleness, softness and tranquillizing meditative qualities. Tai Chi has a significant effect in combating ageing effects by compacting bones and strengthening joints due to the demands of perfect body balance and the precision of placing the feet. Tai Chi is also getting increasingly popular in the west along with Qi Gong.

If you want to learn Tai Chi properly, it is of utmost importance to find an authentic teacher.

There are plenty of unscrupulous charlatans around trying to make money from this profitable market. The most popular forms of Tai Chi are Yang Style, Chan or Chen Style, Wu (pronounced as Ng in Cantonese) Style, another Wu Style (Wu meaning martial, pronounced as Mo in Cantonese), Sun Style, Fu Style and the modern Beijing short form based on Yang Style. If people tell you that they are teaching another style of Tai Chi rather than the ones mentioned above, beware; in nine cases out of ten, they are phony. During the 1970s, when Bruce Lee was first introduced to the west, some impostor sprang up from nowhere teaching pseudo Taoist Arts and Lee-style Tai Chi in a worldwide network.

Authentic Tai Chi must comprise both single and double pushing hand exercises. The double pushing hand exercise is a very complicated two-person form that most impostors are not able to duplicate by learning from books. A student needs to practise double pushing hand with a master to understand the secrets of using soft strength and Qi. Such initiation of strength and Qi is called feeding strength. Authentic Tai Chi teachers must be able to demonstrate the hidden soft strength, which may enable them to repulse someone across a room with a seemingly soft push.

Tai Chi is best practised in the open air, such as a park or in your garden.

Qi Gong or Chi Kung means Qi exercise. There are two formats of Qi Gong, active (Dong) and inactive (Jing). The active format is similar to yoga exercises and the inactive format is performed in meditative postures. Some of the active exercises are derived from the complementary exercises, such as those described in this book. Qi Gong is a healing art of two dimensions. Qi Gong can be practised for convalescence and it is most beneficial for patients regaining strength and recuperating from an illness. A Qi Gong master can direct the Universal Energy Qi to heal the sick and wounded. As Qi Gong and Tai Chi are also from Taoist origins, practising these arts will indeed greatly benefit the advancement of the Alchemy Meditation. Qi Gong and Tai Chi are fascinating subjects.

MEDITATION AND DAILY LIFE

Once a young Ch'an (Zen) disciple asked his master about the secret of attaining enlightenment. His master told him quietly, 'Attention!' The disciple was puzzled and replied, 'I do not understand, master.' The master smiled and shouted strongly, 'Attention! Attention! Attention!' The disciple scratched his head and said to his master, 'But I still do not understand what you are referring to, venerable one.' The master replied, 'My son, you are not paying any attention at all.' He then closed his eyes and went into his meditation.

Meditation does not merely confine itself to the half-hour or one-hour daily ritual of special posture and mental exercise. The ritual of quietude, internalization, introspection and energy circulation is undoubtedly a very important part of your spiritual training. However, meditation is a continuous attention towards all things and a constant awareness towards every moment in your life. It does not, however, mean that we live our everyday lives in a permanent altered stated of consciousness. Even if you are a monk or a hermit, you need to come out of your meditation sometimes to eat, drink, urinate and defecate. When you have fine-tuned your perception, you will realize the utilization of two kinds of attention in your daily life.

One kind of attention is to deal with your everyday life and the other kind is your internal meditative awareness. Once you are proficient with the art of meditation, the two kinds of attention will be interwoven with each other. Your attention toward your external life will become more acute, more perceptive and more connective with both your external and your internal world.

Your awareness of energy circulation on the meridians and internalization will carry on during your wakened consciousness, although they are not as acute as during the meditation practice. Part of your meditative awareness will become an expanded awareness and a more perceptive cognition during your everyday life.

We live in a modern culture of self-centred and limited views manifesting within our individual finite worlds. Most of us lead our lives under very rigid daily structures in specific time slots. We have a very short attention span towards our everyday external activities. We spend much of our lifetime repeating the same daily routines, such as when to get up in the morning, what clothes to put on, what shopping to get, what bill to pay, and what TV programme to watch, without paying any attention to the action. If your attention is constantly drawn toward the same pattern of behaviour, your tasks will eventually become stale, uncreative and meaningless repetitions.

Meditation expands your perception, rekindles your awareness and sharpens your attention beyond your habits. When you reconnect yourself internally, your inner awareness will overlap your external awareness. Once you have mastered such mindfulness, while you are sitting down, you will be sensitive to your sitting posture, to your buttocks being in contact with the chair, to the direction you are facing and the details of the environment. While you are walking, you will be conscious of your steps, your body's coordination, your timing and so on. Every simple daily task will become more enlarged, more focused, more meaningful and more connected with your inner being. Your senses toward everything in the external world will also be imbued with more clarity, more colour, more vibrancy and more sensuality in every way than how you perceived them prior to practising meditation. When you have a higher level of awareness, you will become more intuitive, more perceptive, more empathetic, more sensitive, more compassionate and, finally, more in tune with your external environment.

LIVE A PHILOSOPHICAL LIFE

The *Oxford English Dictionary* defines philosophy as the study of the fundamental nature of knowledge, reality and existence. It is also described as a theory or attitude that guides one's behaviour. Indeed, philosophy arises from the primal curiosity of mankind searching for meanings to life and death, creation and the universal truth of the cosmos. Philosophy shapes man's behaviour and a nation's ethics. The evolution of a civilized society is based on the foundation values set by religious beliefs and philosophical principles. Philosophy defines truth. Truth defines principles. Principles shape morality and morality refines spirituality.

If man follows and espouses Taoist principles, he lives a philosophical, moralistic and spiritual life. He lives a life that is based on the noble qualities of modesty, tolerance, meekness, patience, kindness, diligence, preservation, tranquillity and compassion. These benevolent attributes and high inspirations command harmony and a peaceful life. Taoists perceive being kind to others as being kind to oneself and one's body. Being kind to yourself and your body brings about physical and emotional concord that promotes good health and longevity. While Taoist philosophy is the soul, Alchemy Meditation is the heart and healthy living is the body of the Taoist spiritual path. All three need to go hand in hand, in unison, and they are equally important for attaining Immortality.

To live a philosophical life is to follow the greatness of Tao:

• To have flexibility of ever becoming and ever transforming

• To be spontaneous and to adapt to changes

• To contain and to dispose at will

• To live without ownership

• To give without wishing for return

• To succeed without seeking approval

• To act without lordship

• To be fair, kind, compassionate and non-judgemental

• To follow the middle way and to practise the principle of non-action (Wu Wei)

• To observe, to study and to learn from those with great virtues

Finally, abide to the Universal Taoist Law of 'cycle of return' or 'Yin and Yang harmonization'. This law is fundamentally the same as the law of Karma in Buddhism or the principle of Christianity's 'whatever you sow, you shall reap'.

We are what we think. With our thoughts, we manifest the nature of what we are and how we shape the world. Our desires and intentions arise from our internal world and determine the making or destruction of our external world. A philosopher once said, 'When I move my finger the whole world moves along with me.' History has revealed to us time and time again how one man's thought could mobilize mass belief, emotions and sentiments in the name of personal ego, nationalism or religion leading to racial hatred, genocide, war and massive destruction.

Positive thinking and creative ideas promote progress and harmony for the common good. Negative intentions and destructive thoughts yield disharmony and annihilation to others and oneself. Hatred can breed more hatred. Retribution, violence and loathing create the endless cycle of revenge, disharmony and destruction. We are all responsible and answerable to our own thoughts and deeds in this life and hereafter. Do good and goodness will revisit you. Do evil and evil returns. This applies to yourself, your environment, your edification, your intentions, your body, your mind, your spirit and all things that are associated with you and your life. You are the creator of yourself, your life, your world and your destiny. May you create a healthy, productive, positive, enriching, happy and long spiritual life.

Index

Acknowledgements

I would like to express my gratitude to my Hard Style Shaolin Kung Fu Master, Chang Yong Fai, whom I regarded as a father as well as my teacher, my Soft Style Taoist martial arts and Qi Gong teacher, Wu Bing Yin, a very close friend, whom I looked upon as an elder brother. I am also thankful to Dr Lu who initiated my understanding of Taoism and opened my mind to see with insight. Also special thanks are due to Dr Paul Brunton (an English philosopher and mystic), Lama Anagarika Govinda (a Tantric Cleric) and Tien Chuang Yang (a contemporary Taoist Cleric) who shared much of their spiritual knowledge in their rich and prolific textual work.

Executive Editor Brenda Rosen
Managing Editor Clare Churly
Executive Art Editor Sally Bond
Designer Julie Francis
Picture Researcher Vickie Walters
Production Controller Simone Nauerth

PICTURE ACKNOWLEDGEMENTS
Corbis 65, 66, 105. **Getty Images**/San An 91;
/Pieter Estersohn 104; /Raymond Gehman 89;
/Ghislain & Marie David de Lossy 103; /Keren Su 88.
Octopus Publishing Group Limited 9, 30, 33,
34, 36 left, 37 left, 37 right, 38 centre, 38 bottom
right, 38 bottom left, 39 background, 40, 43, 48 left,
48 right, 49, 50 left, 50 right, 51 left, 51 right, 52 left,
52 right, 53, 54 left, 54 right, 55 left, 55 right, 56 left,
56 right, 57, 58 left, 58 right, 59 left, 59 right, 60, 61,
64, 68 left, 68 right, 69 left, 69 right, 72 right, 73, 73
left, 74 left, 74 right, 74 centre left, 74 centre right,
75 left, 75 centre left, 82, 99, 100 centre, 100
bottom, 101, 102, 109 top, 109 bottom, 118, 122,
127, 130, 134, 136, 137, 139; /Frank Adam 95 top;
/Colin Bowling 106, 107, 108; /Mike Hemsley 120,
121, 125; /William Lingwood 95, 111 bottom; /Leo
Mason 98; /Sean Myers 94; /Lis Parsons 93 bottom,
111 top, 119; /William Reavell 92, 93 top, 110;
/Roger Stowell 119 bottom; /Mark Winwood 35, 35
top; 96. **Photodisc** 2, 7, 10, 23, 44–45, 83, 112,
114–115. **Werner Forman Archive**/National
Gallery, Prague 24